NOTRE DAME
FIGHTING IRISH
NATIONAL CHAMPIONS

1924	10	0	0
1929	9	0	0
1930	10	0	0
1943	9	1	0
1946	8	0	1
1947	9	0	0
1949	10	0	0
1966	9	0	1
1973	11	0	0
1977	11	1	0
1988	12	0	0

PLAY LIKE A CHAMPION TODAY

Other books by Joe Garner:

We Interrupt This Broadcast

And The Crowd Goes Wild

And The Fans Roared

ECHOES OF NOTRE DAME FOOTBALL

Great and Memorable Moments of the Fighting Irish

JOE GARNER ▪ **REGIS PHILBIN** ▪ **ARA PARSEGHIAN** ▪ **JOE THEISMANN**

Narrator   *Foreword*   *Afterword*

SOURCEBOOKS MEDIAFUSION™
AN IMPRINT OF SOURCEBOOKS, INC.®
NAPERVILLE, ILLINOIS

Published by Sourcebooks, Inc.
P.O. Box 4410, Naperville, Illinois 60567-4410
(630) 961-3900
FAX: (630) 961-2168
www.sourcebooks.com

Library of Congress Cataloging-in-Publication Data

Garner, Joe.
    Echoes of Notre Dame football: great and memorable moments of the Fighting Irish / by Joe Garner.
        p. cm.
    ISBN 1-57071-763-X (alk. paper)
    1. Notre Dame Fighting Irish (Football team)—History. 2. University of Notre Dame—Football—History. I. Title.

GV958.U54 G37 2001
796.332'63'0977289—dc21   2001032243

Printed and bound in the United States of America
QG   10 9 8 7 6 5 4 3 2 1

To the fans of the Fighting Irish—
the keepers of the tradition, legend,
and spirit of Notre Dame

Table of Contents

Introduction

If I hadn't felt intimidated enough already by my decision to do a book about Notre Dame football's legendary moments, the task seemed even more overwhelming shortly after I sat down to have lunch with Joe Doyle, South Bend's most notable Notre Dame football historian. Joe's been writing about Notre Dame football for fifty-one years and was the sports editor for the *South Bend Tribune* for thirty. He even became friends with Rockne's predecessor Jess Harper in Harper's later years. But from Leahy's era to the present, Joe's expert knowledge is not only unmatched, it's also firsthand.

I was pleased that Joe had accepted my invitation to meet. I think in some way I was hoping for validation. But no sooner had Joe and I exchanged greetings than he assailed me with a rhetorical comment that shook my confidence to the core: "Well, just what we need, another book about Notre Dame football." In rapid succession, the wind in my sails began to calm—then fade.

After the release of my two previous sports compilations, *And The Crowd Goes Wild* and *And The Fans Roared*, I discovered just how passionate and critical sports fans could be. But Joe taught me that, by comparison, the intensity of the Notre Dame spirit is nearly immeasurable, and capturing it in each story would be integral in creating an exhilarating experience for the reader.

I will never forget my first of several pilgrimages to South Bend in January of 2000. I had heard the stories of the mystique of the campus. I knew it was where Rockne, Gipp, and Leahy once walked. I had read of Ara Parseghian feeling a tingle go up his spine the first time he saw the sun gleaming off the Golden Dome. But it wasn't until I turned up Notre Dame Avenue that I truly felt what to that moment I had only heard and read about.

I pulled my rental car into the parking space at The Morris Inn, the University's on-campus hotel, and began walking toward the lobby. Despite the cold winter wind whipping across my face and cutting through my less-than-adequate overcoat, I stood in awe as I looked out across the main quadrant of the campus. The "God-quad" as students have lovingly dubbed it, is the oldest quadrant, and majestically sitting at the far end is the main administration building where "Our Lady" stands gazing down from atop the Golden Dome. As I was taking in the sight, I wondered if I was up to the task of taking on such a legend.

In September of that year, I joined my friend Tony Zirille for the much-ballyhooed Notre Dame vs. Nebraska game. We started the day by participating in the revered gameday ritual: the tailgate party. This was much more than your garden-variety bratwurst sacrifice atop charcoal-filled Weber grills. In the parking lot adjoining the stadium, there were rows and rows of RVs, cars, SUVs, and forty-one corporate tents spread out on the practice field. We enjoyed the hospitality of the Sullivan family party. Mrs. Sullivan served up her homemade mostaccioli, and the wine bottles never seemed to empty. And "Big Ed" Sullivan (class of '57) regaled us with wonderful stories of past gridiron battles when he and teammates Paul Hornung and Dick Lynch ruled the field at Notre Dame Stadium.

Once inside "The House That Rockne Built," I couldn't help but feel that mortal boundaries are mystically transcended on gameday. I could almost see the ghosts of the players, students, and fans of the past commingling with the players, students, and fans of the present, all reveling in the possibility that today's game could become legend. Although I saw a great game, I won't talk about the outcome here because the wound is still a little too raw for most diehard "Domers." It was a thrill nonetheless.

During my next trip to Notre Dame, I immersed myself in the University's archive on the sixth floor of the Hesburgh Memorial Library. I touched the past, leafing through mountains of photographs, articles, and memorabilia that would help me bring the more than one hundred–year history and spirit of Notre Dame football to life.

Now it was time to select the stories. I consulted a team of journalists, some of whom report on the Irish for various publications; solicited the fans' favorites through my publisher's website; discussed potential events with members of the University's administration; and conferred with Notre Dame's Heisman Trophy winners including Johnny Lattner, Johnny Lujack, and John Huarte.

We live in an era where how we *heard* an event on the radio or *watched* it unfold on television has become inextricably linked with our memory of the moment. In keeping with my style of storytelling, I decided to include the actual play-by-play broadcast for each story chronicled in the book. Hearing Joe Boland, Jim Gibbons, and Tony Roberts call these thrilling moments is like hearing a favorite old song, it unlocks the emotions fans have stored with the memory of each of these timeless events. Unfortunately, I discovered that the broadcasts of the Notre Dame–Army game of 1924 and the Notre Dame–Oklahoma game of 1957 no longer exist. I was honored and thrilled when lifelong Notre Dame fan Martin Sheen agreed to read excerpts of Grantland Rice's famed 1924 "Four Horsemen" article, and Notre Dame running back Dick Lynch recounted his celebrated touchdown run against Oklahoma, in lieu of these lost broadcasts.

From the moment I decided to do this book, there was only one person I had in mind to give voice to the stories on the accompanying CDs. Whether setting the scene for "Gameday," describing the miracle kick of Harry O', or the last-second heroics of Shawn Wooden against Florida State, Regis Philbin's love of Notre Dame football is well known, and his passion comes through in his narration.

While I hope that these stories, photographs, and broadcasts evoke many wonderful memories, I also hope that they provide a few surprises. *Echoes of Notre Dame Football* is a scrapbook of wonderful memories. I hope it provides a link from one generation of Notre Dame fans to the next. And hopefully, it will become the "one more book about Notre Dame football" that Joe Doyle and fans of the Fighting Irish will appreciate and enjoy.

Foreword
by Ara Parseghian

In my high school yearbook, under what my future might be, it read, "will become the coach of Notre Dame."

I can't remember a time when I wasn't aware of Notre Dame football. Growing up in Akron, Ohio, during the '20s and '30s, Notre Dame football under Knute Rockne was preeminent. I was just eight years old when Rockne died in that plane crash in Kansas in 1931, but I have vivid memories of newspaper boys coming down the street selling "Extras" after it happened. The success that Rockne was able to generate, and the class with which he did it, left a strong impression on me.

After my own pro career playing for the Cleveland Browns was cut short due to an injury, I began pursuing a coaching career, first at Miami of Ohio and then at Northwestern. To that point, all of Notre Dame's football coaches had been graduates of the university, and all except Rockne were Catholics. I was neither. But at Northwestern I did get to coach against Notre Dame—we played them four times, home and away, and we won all four games. So I got to know Notre Dame's president, Father Theodore Hesburgh C.S.C., and the vice president responsible for the athletic program, Father Edmond Joyce C.S.C. When Notre Dame decided to pick a new coach in 1963, I threw my hat in the ring. One thing led to another, and I got the job.

By this time, I'd been a head football coach for fourteen years, eight of them in the Big Ten, so I figured that I knew what I was in for. I was wrong. The first time I came up Notre Dame Avenue as head coach is when it really hit me. As I caught my first glimpse of the Golden Dome, I felt an electric charge go right up my back with the sudden realization of the enormity of responsibility to a winning tradition that I'd been familiar with all my life.

again. There were so many people there I couldn't believe it. It's that kind of support that would allow us to win big time.

Notre Dame had not had a winning season in the prior five years. So expectations weren't great at first. But once I got there I realized there was talent on the team—it had just been misplaced. My staff and I began making adjustments, the team got on a roll and won some games, and all of the sudden we resurrected the whole Notre Dame spirit. The next year, 1964, was a very exciting year because of the dramatic change. And it was a little overwhelming too, because we'd never experienced anything like it.

Remember, this was back when Notre Dame was an all-male school, and it was run almost like a military academy. At pep rallies before each game, fans would fill up the old field house and it was the darndest thing you'd ever seen. We'd be up in the balcony and it was wall-to-wall people and their arms are flying up in the air and chanting, "We're number one. We're number one…" The excitement that went with that first year, and everyone rallying together, made the whole staff and everyone in our department feel like we were Notre Dame men too. There was a great *esprit de corps*, and you couldn't help but be a part of it.

It didn't take me long to recognize how different things were. At Northwestern, we were recruiting football players from about a five hundred–mile radius of the school. At Notre Dame, I was recruiting from the whole United States. Of course you don't get every kid you want, because now you're competing with the big state universities—Notre Dame or Alabama, Notre Dame or Michigan, Notre Dame or Texas, Notre Dame or Southern California. Back when I was at Miami of Ohio, I used to sell athletes on their future in that state. Now I was selling them on a future that was national: "After you graduate, you can call from anywhere in this country and you can have people who will be of help to you." That was one difference.

Then there was the enthusiasm. I began working at Notre Dame in December of 1963. Two months later I got a call from the students in Sorin Hall, one of the dormitories. They wanted to have a pep rally on the steps of the building—in February. There were several inches of snow on the ground. I didn't really think that anyone would show up. I was wrong

The idea behind Notre Dame football is very simple, as Father Hesburgh expressed it to me in our first interview: we want excellence in all fields at the university. And he also told me this: as long as you abide by the rules and regulations of the NCAA, you'll have me 100 percent behind you. But if you violate those rules, you could go undefeated and be national champions and you'd still be out of here. That stuck in my mind too. There's no reason why you can't abide by the rules, do everything right, and still be successful, and that's where Father Hesburgh and Father Joyce were coming from. Now, some die-hard Notre Dame followers do not always share that view! But I knew Father Hesburgh's word was as good as his bond, so I never worried about it.

I know there are some fervent followers who also think that Notre Dame football is sometimes guided by a religious authority even higher than Father Hesburgh's. Certainly it's wonderful to have the "Touchdown Jesus" mural towering over the field as part of the Notre Dame tradition. But that image can't block or tackle. God doesn't favor one team over another—this is a game to be played. But what goes with that at Notre Dame is a terrific enthusiasm and spirit, and the very thing that religion deals with—faith. So when you combine all of that, it's a powerful package.

I coached for eleven years at Notre Dame, which was also Knute Rockne's tenure, and Frank Leahy's tenure. We had great success, but the emotional toll became draining. Still, it was not an easy decision to leave. I wrestled with it for about a year and a half before I decided to leave coaching behind, and I have no regrets about that. But I wouldn't trade one minute of those eleven years at Notre Dame for anything.

Many of the most thrilling moments in Notre Dame football history are part of my life. Some I first heard of while growing up as a child; others I cheered on as a fan. After I became coach, some took shape before my eyes.

Reliving them all through the stories and pictures of this book, along with the dramatic audio broadcasts on the CDs, I'm reminded again of the awesome responsibility that comes with upholding this unique tradition.

Since retiring from Notre Dame in 1975, I've been asked many times why I never returned to coach college football somewhere else. This book helps explain why. For me, after you've coached college football at Notre Dame, there's really nowhere else to go.

The fact is, I've never really left Notre Dame. I moved to South Bend with my family in 1964, and I've been here ever since. Today I live five miles from the stadium. From my office, which is closer, I can see the Golden Dome. When I look out the window in that direction, I'm reminded of my high school yearbook prediction and how lucky I am that it actually came true.

Ara Parseghian

ECHOES OF NOTRE DAME FOOTBALL

Gameday

"Notre Dame football weekends are tightly scripted extravaganzas that set the standard for football weekends everywhere, designed by people with an attachment to sacramental rituals."

—Thomas O'Meara, O.P.
Professor of Theology, University of Notre Dame

It's Saturday—gameday. The Indiana morning sky is crisp and blue. The air, a sweet blend of autumn scents with freshly-lit charcoal grills. The rising sun reflecting off the Golden Dome, as the grass on the quad glistens with morning dew.

Today, the campus comes alive with a unique reverence for things past and anticipation of things to come. Today, students prepare to stand in their seats in "The House That Rockne Built," and cheer on their Fighting Irish like a century of students have done before them.

"Gameday!" yells the first one up in his campus dorm as reveille. "Gameday!" they remind themselves as they don their lucky ball caps and paint shamrocks on their faces. "Gameday!" as they pass in the dining halls at breakfast. "Gameday!" they chant as they parade from campus out to the stadium parking lots, to join the tailgating thousands who have been arriving from across the nation since Thursday. Today's celebrations will become tomorrow's ritual.

Today, college buddies from across the country wake up the echoes of college days past and reunite with high-fives and bear hugs. Through the window of a minivan draped in blue and gold, a little boy spies the Golden Dome for the first time as his family arrives on campus. Today is the day Irish eyes smile the most; when those with an

"ND" emblazoned on their sweatshirts and on their souls alike will answer the call of "Touchdown Jesus." It's gameday at Notre Dame.

For those past their college prime, the annual pilgrimage has been marked on calendars for

(left to right) Gameday at Notre Dame Stadium ■ *The grandstand ticket office in 1894*

—FOOTBALL.—For some days previous to Wednesday great interest had been manifested by our students in the football game which had been arranged between the teams of the Universities of Michigan and Notre Dame. It was not considered a match contest, as the home team had been organized only a few weeks, and the Michigan boys, the champions of the West, came more to instruct them in the points of the Rugby game than to win fresh laurels. The visitors arrived over the Michigan Central RR., Wednesday morning, and were at once taken in charge by a committee of students. After spending a few hours in "taking in" the surroundings, they donned their uniforms of spotless white and appeared upon the Seniors' campus. Owing to the recent thaw, the field was damp and muddy; but nothing daunted, the boys "went in," and soon Harless' new suit appeared as though it had imbibed some of its wearer's affinity for the soil of Notre Dame. At first, to render our players more familiar with the game, the teams were chosen irrespective of college. After some minutes' play, the game was called, and each took his position as follows:

UNIV. OF M.—*Full Back:* J. L. Duffy; *Half Backs:* J. E. Duffy, E. McPheran; *Quarter Back:* R. T. Farrand; *Centre Rush:* W. W. Harless; *Rush Line:* F. Townsend, E. M. Sprague F. H. Knapp, W. Fowler, G. W. De Haven, M. Wade.

UNIV. OF N. D.—*Full Back:* H. Jewett; *Half Backs:* J. Cusack, H. Luhn; *Quarter Back:* G. Cartier; *Centre Rush:* G. A. Houck; *Rush Line:* F. Fehr, P. Nelson, B. Sawkins, W. Springer, T. O'Regan, P. P. Maloney.

On account of time, only a part of one inning was played, and resulted in a score of 8 to 0 in favor of the visitors. The game was interesting, and, notwithstanding the slippery condition of the ground, the Ann Arbor boys gave a fine exhibition of skilful playing. This occasion has started an enthusiastic football boom, and it is hoped that coming years will witness a series of these contests. After a hearty dinner, Rev. President Walsh thanked the Ann Arbor team for their visit, and assured them of the cordial reception that would always await them at Notre Dame. At 1 o'clock carriages were taken for Niles, and amidst rousing cheers the University of Michigan football team departed, leaving behind them a most favorable impression.

An article describing the first football game played at Notre Dame in 1887

months. Notre Dame is a Mecca of sorts. It is a school where so many alumni return to campus for home games each year that the school does not designate a homecoming weekend. For alumni, family, fans, and Notre Dame's famed "subway alumni"—a constituency of Irish fans first developed when Knute Rockne took the team to cities like New York, Philadelphia, Pittsburgh, and Los Angeles—gameday is a scripted blend of rite and ritual in which every scene is as critical to the day as the game itself

Those who will send their volley cheers the highest take their place amidst the green, blue, and gold waves of pregame tailgaters. Tailgating is legendary at Notre Dame, where portable feasts serve brats and crème brûlée on the same Fighting Irish plate, and where Irish toasts are chased with a handful of gourmet blue and gold M&Ms. A game of touch football breaks out, but soon ends when an errant pass grazes the hood of a parked car across the way. In the midst of it all, an old Notre Dame family from the East Coast is sharing their annual gameday spread with passersby.

Not far away, a group of Saturday afternoon bachelors from South Chicago sit atop their coolers, reminiscing about their favorite Notre Dame football moments. They come from all over, represent every walk of life, spanning the economic strata. Today, everyone is Irish.

The smell of cigars fills the air as another costumed leprechaun passes by. A kilted bagpipe player is taking requests, and soon a rendition of "Danny Boy" turns into another spirited round of "The Notre Dame Victory March." CD players and car horns echoing those same songs provide a backdrop for the sea of RVs, cars, and SUVs. It is a forum of tradition that rivals the excitement of the game itself.

As the noise level outside rises, inside the chapel the heroes of the day sit in silence and prayer. The team Mass on gameday is mandatory, a tradition

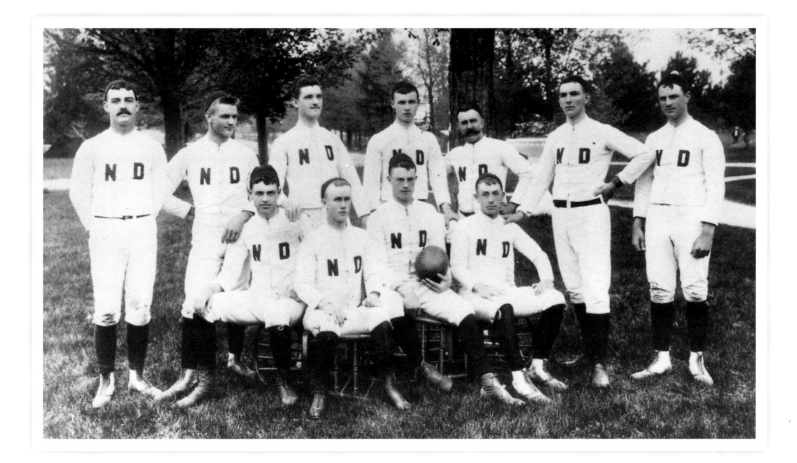

that dates back to a time when most of the players were sons of Irish, German, Polish, and Italian Catholic immigrants, when Notre Dame football on Saturdays gave a sense of identity and pride to a Catholic working class across the country. Today, the team Mass remains the private domain of the coaches, players, and presiding clergy, who blend the readings of the day with the team's task at hand. Spiritually fired, dressed in coat and tie, and with gym bags in hand, the privilege of gameday is theirs as the players part the sea of devout fans on their walk through campus to the stadium.

For many fans, gameday rituals are more reflective. Some stop at the Grotto, a replica of the candle-laden tribute to the Virgin Mary in Lourdes, France, to light a candle for a loved one, or to humbly request a win for the home team. Some attend one of the many gameday Masses offered in the dorms

around campus. Others will return to campus to the Sacred Heart Basilica after the game, where it's said that the pews are always as packed as the stadium seats and through which ten thousand people will pass on any given home game Saturday.

Not to be missed is the annual trip to Dad's old dorm, and the obligatory visit to the trophy case where his name still holds its proud place among his teammates. Or the walk around St. Mary's Lake, reliving Grandpa's story about the time he was tossed into its icy waters, penance for having overslept the welcome home tribute for the football team at the train station.

Many will pass venerate statues throughout the campus, faith-filled art six days a week, but each given a slightly irreverent and different identity on gameday. Among them perhaps, the statue of Moses

Notre Dame took the field in 1888 with team members (back row, left to right) J.L. Hepburn, G. Houck, E.A. Sawkins, F. Fehr, P. Nelson, G. Melady, F. Springer; (front row) H.M. Jewett, J.E. Cusack, H.B. Luhn, E. Prudhoome.

A view of the old Notre Dame stadium

in front of the library with tablets in one hand and the index finger on the other extended high in the air is transformed into "We're No. 1 Moses." Most famous of all is the mosaic mural of Jesus Christ, arms outstretched and surrounded by saints and scholars that adorns the exterior wall of the fourteen-story Hesburgh Memorial Library. "Touchdown Jesus" is visible to many of the Irish faithful packed into Notre Dame Stadium.

Anticipation now peaks at the crystallizing moment of the day. The band assembles for its home game concert on the steps of the administration building beneath the Golden Dome. Every tuba, cymbal, and brass button must shine as radiantly as the dome above. The day's overture begins, from a band whose roots date back even beyond the school's first exhibition football game.

America's oldest collegiate marching band played on these same steps in November 1887, as the first student fans joined in singing "Rah, Rah, Nostra Domina." Today, it's "Cheer, Cheer for Ol' Notre Dame" that's waking up the echoes of Notre Dame football.

Inspection of the band and Irish Guard follows. Before them, thousands line the central campus walkways that lead toward the stadium. The cheerleaders and the student leprechaun mascot lead the way. Next follow the quick, high, precise steps of the kilt-clad and legendary Irish Guard. "This is the first official act of war," reveals one alumnus of the band's march to the stadium.

Now, as the band steps off section-by-section, row-by-row, the crowd erupts into a fist-pumping,

NOTRE DAME MUST BE PLAYIN' FOOTBALL AGAIN.

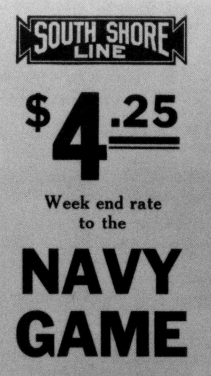

SOUTH SHORE LINE

$4.25

Week end rate to the

NAVY GAME

Take the South Shore Line (trains every hour on the hour —LaSalle and Michigan, across from where the Notre Dame street car stops) direct to the Stadium. Special $4.25 round trip week end rate—good on all trains from noon Friday, October 12, to and including midnight train out of Chicago Sunday night, October 14. 7 A. M. flyer out of South Bend the day of the game will go to Roosevelt Road (Stadium gate) in 2 hours—carries dining car. 10 A. M. train carries parlor. Call Traffic Department, 2-5764, or Ticket Agent, 3-3111 or 3-3112.

South Shore Lines

Irish-whooping frenzy of euphoric cheers. It echoes across campus. "Goooooo Irish!" the crowd chants with happy excitement, "and at the same time," admits one alum, "it brings tears to your eyes." Some rush to strategic vantage points so as not to miss the band turn its single corner en route into the stadium. Most fall in step behind the band, sons and daughters on their dads' shoulders, boyfriends and girlfriends hand-in-hand, alumni and fans from all walks of life, all stepping to the same pounding beat. They all savor the crusade-like march through the throngs of cheering fans in anticipation of a victory in which they will share and remember always.

The stadium swells with invitation as the fans pour in. Shoulder-to-shoulder, they make their way up the ramp from the darkened concourse into the stadium. The cheers of the crowd grow louder and the day seemingly glows brighter. Upon entering the stadium, the colors are blinding. Small patches of the visiting team's colors contrast against the blanket of Irish blue and green. The battle flags of the season's opponents wave in the autumn breeze atop the stadium walls. And someone named George C. is already proposing to someone named Katy S. on an airplane banner circling above.

(left to right) Even early on, Notre Dame faithful were known for cheering on the Irish no matter where they were playing.
■ *A newspaper ad offers special rates for Chicagoans heading to the Notre Dame–Navy game.*

Constructed in 1930, "The House That Rock Built" is indeed alive and well. It is pulsed by those who profess to bleed blue and gold, and beats with the heart of its immortal champions. As the band plays "America the Beautiful," the freshly striped, green grass field evokes memories of heroics past.

Where Rockne sent his boys to battle.

Where Leahy's lads dominated college football like no other.

Where Parseghian, Devine, and Holtz vanquished their foes.

Where Bertelli, Lujack, Hart, Lattner, Hornung, Huarte, and Brown proved to be the top college players in the country.

Where Theismann, Montana, Oliver, and Ismail shook down the thunder time and again.

Now as the Fighting Irish leave their locker room and head to the field to meet their foe, they pass beneath the sign that reminds them of the torch they now carry, "Play Like a Champion Today."

Their still unblemished golden helmets sparkle in the afternoon sun. Joining the ghosts of Notre Dame's past, the stadium is packed with cheering fans, and all are on their feet. The anticipation grows as the kicker places the ball on the tee. Everything seems possible at kickoff in Notre Dame

Notre Dame's tradition of football excellence and gameday enthusiasm dates back to the late 1800s and early 1900s.

(top to bottom) *A salute from the Irish Guard* ■ *The Irish marching band performs at halftime.* ■ *The Fighting Irish marching band shows its spirit.*

Stadium. The students are now screaming and circling their arms in unison as the kicker addresses the ball and sends it skyward. The roar of the crowd grows even louder.

Today you may see your favorite player have his greatest moment. Today you may share in the greatest of comebacks with your child or your best friend at your side. You may retell the story of this particular day and this particular game for the rest of your life. All of Notre Dame's history and lore, and all of the traditions and rituals evoke in fans, coaches, and players alike a genuine belief and confidence that on any given autumn Saturday the Irish can accomplish the impossible.

Every single moment at Notre Dame Stadium adds to the rich montage of more than a century of football greatness. And today, you become a part of it all. It's gameday.

Knute Rockne, All-American

"I'm a ringmaster. If I give a good show they like me; if I don't, they'll be barking at my heels—alumni, newspapers, students, and the great public at large."

—Knute Rockne

Notre Dame is replete with tradition and larger-than-life figures. But since its founding, no figure has loomed larger than Knute Rockne. What makes his story most remarkable is that he reached the pinnacle of national fame while coaching football at a comparatively small school in the small midwestern community of South Bend, Indiana. But it was his charismatic personality and success on the football field that captured the imagination of the country, making him a beloved and revered figure to this day.

This American hero, whose first name, when pronounced correctly, sounds like "Ka-noot," was born Knute Kenneth Rockne on March 4, 1888, in the small mountain town of Voss, Norway. When Knute was just five years old, his father Lars, a Norwegian carriage-maker, immigrated with his wife, son, and three daughters to America. They settled in a middle-class suburb of Chicago. Knute participated in all sports, but was not naturally gifted as an athlete. He left high school and went to work in the post office. At his sister's encouragement, Knute decided to go to college. Over the next four years, he saved his money, hoping to enter the University of Illinois. Instead, Knute made the fateful decision to join a friend and enroll at Notre Dame.

Knute Rockne became a fine student, majoring in chemistry. He was a star on the track team, even setting an indoor world record in pole vaulting. He acted in theater and played the flute. But it was on the football field that Rockne showed his true genius. Measuring just 5-foot, 8-inches, 165 pounds, coach Jess Harper positioned him at end, and later said Rockne was one of the greatest that he had ever seen play the position.

The most famous myth to arise from Rockne's playing days at Notre Dame is that he and teammate Charles "Gus" Dorais invented the forward pass. Most football historians credit Eddie Cochems, head coach at St. Louis University from 1906 to 1908, with being the first to implement the passing game. These were the formative years of college football. In 1910, in an effort to curb the brutality of the game, which was primarily a succession of ground attacks resulting in considerable injuries, the Rules Committee of the IAA (the predecessor of the NCAA) loosened regulations on the use of the forward pass, along with increasing the number of downs to four. The forward pass, legal but seldom used, suddenly became a weapon brandished by every serious college football program. None used it to greater effect than Rockne and Dorais.

In the summer before the 1913 season, Rockne and Dorais, Notre Dame's quarterback, headed off to

(left to right) Knute Rockne runs after catching a Gus Dorais pass against Army in 1913. ■ Rockne served as team captain for Notre Dame during the 1913 season.

(top to bottom) Rockne looks on in practice. ■ Rockne practices blocking with one of his players.

Cedar Point, Ohio, to work as lifeguards and bus-boys. They packed a football with their swimtrunks and, in their spare time, played catch on the beach. Rockne, who had a habit of catching the ball in his stomach, wanted to learn to catch it with his hands. When the boys returned to campus in the fall, Harper worked on an array of Dorais–Rockne pass patterns.

When Notre Dame met the Army Cadets on November 1, 1913, Dorais got in the huddle in the first quarter and said, "Let's open it up." Nobody knew what he meant more than his buddy, Rockne. The rest of the world found out when Rockne caught a forty-yard touchdown pass during under-dog Notre Dame's 35 to 13 romp.

The Notre Dame football program, respected but hardly revered, had gotten its first real taste of national exposure. And it would linger, mostly because of the flavor Rockne added to the sport, the university, the city of South Bend, and the sidewalks on which he stepped.

Following graduation, and after four years as assistant coach, Knute Rockne replaced Jess Harper as Notre Dame's head football coach in 1918. For the next thirteen years, Rockne amassed an astonishing record of 105–12–5. His .881 winning percentage still ranks at the top of the list for college and pro coaches.

Rockne also introduced intersectional rivalries in an era when traveling was a chore. Traveling to places as far east as New York, Pittsburgh, and Philadelphia, and as far west as Los Angeles, Rockne nurtured a constituency of fans made up of Catholics—Polish and Irish immigrants—who adopted the Fighting Irish as their own, a fan base now commonly referred to as "subway alumni." He employed the first set of "shock troops," a full unit of substitutes at the start of the game to provide a jolt. He developed the offensive shift after getting the idea while one day watching dancers at a musical. Rockne was to college football what Henry Ford was to automobiles, a

pioneer who dared to think beyond the limits because of his unique blend of passion and pizzazz.

Rockne's ingenuity on the field could only be matched by his motivational tactics off the field. He was not above employing elaborate theatrics and exploiting his own illness, threatening resignation, or fabricating the story of a deathly ill child to motivate his teams to victory. The most famous of his inspiring and emotional locker room pep talks concerned the alleged deathbed request of George Gipp, who died December 14, 1920, of a strep infection, and whom Rockne called the greatest halfback to ever play on his teams.

As Rockne told it, George Gipp feebly turned to Rockne, the man whose keen eye for talent discovered him one day punting the ball in street clothes on the Notre Dame campus, and issued his dying wish. "Some time, Rock, when the team is up against it, when things are wrong and the breaks are beating the boys—tell them to go in there with all

(top to bottom) Rockne poses on the first day of practice in 1930 with players hoping to make the Irish squad. ■ A 1920 photo of Rockne

they've got and win just one for the Gipper. I don't know where I'll be then, Rock. But I'll know about it. And I'll be happy."

Not until eight years later, as the legend goes, did Rockne invoke Gipp's name to the boys of Notre Dame. It was November 10, 1928, and the Irish had lost two of their first six games, sins for which no penance could compensate as far as Notre Dame fans were concerned. Army entered the game unbeaten.

An autographed photo of George Gipp, who was immortalized in Rockne's 1928 "Win One for the Gipper" speech.

Rockne did not arrive unprepared. Whether he actually delivered his stirring speech during pregame remarks or at the half remains uncertain.

"The day before he died," Rockne implored the Irish, his pitch reaching a crescendo, "George Gipp asked me to wait until the situation seemed hopeless—then ask a Notre Dame team to go out and beat Army for him. This is the day, and you are the team!" Silence draped the room, but only for a second. "All of a sudden those players ran out of the dressing room and almost tore the hinges off the door. They were ready to kill someone," former line coach Ed Healy later told reporters. And all that mattered was that an inspired Notre Dame beat Army that day. They won one for the Gipper, 12 to 6.

Perhaps Gipp never made such a request, as some historians have alleged, and even if the speech was so contrived that Rockne confided its contents to a neighbor a week before the game, all that mattered was that Irish players believed Rockne to the last syllable. At Notre Dame, the truth was what Rockne said it was. Nobody doubted him. Nobody questioned him. Nobody dared. From that day forward, defining the spirit of Notre Dame would be easy for future generations.

Despite the demands of coaching at Notre Dame, and often at the objection of the administration, Rockne was involved in numerous entrepreneurial ventures. He wrote a weekly newspaper column. He served as a spokesman for Studebaker, the automaker. He opened a local brokerage firm. He even wrote three books. Simultaneously, he served as Notre Dame's athletic director, business manager, ticket manager, and track coach. Rockne even had a hand in designing what now stands as Notre Dame Stadium, known to many as "the house that Rockne built."

But the breakneck pace nearly broke Rockne. Before the 1929 season, he became seriously ill after being stricken with phlebitis—an inflammation of the veins of the leg. Still, Rockne persisted in his work. He coached practice from the seat of an automobile and used a megaphone to make his points to players. In a game against USC in Chicago, Rockne called the shots from a wheelchair. He eventually recovered from the disease, but remained an incurable workaholic.

Many college football historians consider Rockne's greatest example of coaching to be the 1929 and 1930 seasons. Both resulted in unbeaten records and national titles for Notre Dame. With this success on the gridiron came more and more outside opportunities. It was just such an opportunity that took Rockne out of South Bend for the last time. On March 30, 1931, Rockne was headed to Los Angeles to meet with Universal Pictures about participating in a football-themed movie. After a brief stop in Chicago for dinner, Rockne boarded a train to Kansas City to spend some time with his two sons who were attending prep school. He then was to fly to Los Angeles.

The next day, on March 31, just before taking off, a friend of Rockne's wished him a "soft landing." "You mean 'happy landing,' don't you?" Rockne replied. Just minutes after takeoff, Transcontinental-Western Flight 599 carrying Rockne, five other passengers, and two pilots, flew into a storm. Ice quickly covered the plane, and the wind caused the wings to quake.

The nation responded with shock and sadness at the news of Rockne's tragic death. ■ *(bottom right) The mangled wreckage of Rockne's plane strewn across a farmer's field in Bazaar, Kansas. Eight people perished in the crash; there were no survivors.*

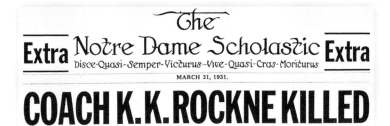

Below, a farmer in a wheat field in Bazaar, Kansas, looked up when he heard a motor sputter and saw the plane falling from the sky. The crash left no survivors.

The news of Rockne's death soon gripped the nation. The reaction was nearly unprecedented. The operators at the *Chicago Tribune* were inundated by so many calls that they began answering with the phrase, "Yes, it's true about Rockne."

Notre Dame's former president John J. Kavanaugh said, "On campus…men with frozen faces looked hard into one another's eyes and passed by unspeaking."

(left to right) Crowds of mourners gathered as the funeral procession passed through campus. ■ Inside the chapel, Notre Dame president Father Charles O'Donnell presided over Rockne's funeral.

Syndicated columnist Will Rogers shared his sense of national tragedy, writing, "We thought it would take a president or a great public man's death to make a whole nation, regardless of age, race, or creed shake their heads in real sorrow and say, 'Ain't it a shame he's gone?' It takes a big calamity to shock a country all at once, but Knute, you did it. You died one of our national heroes. Notre Dame was your address, but every gridiron in America was your home."

In its collective mourning, the nation listened to Rockne's funeral over the CBS Radio network. Members of the championship team served as pallbearers, and others from the class of 1914, among them former roommate and teammate Gus Dorais, served in the honor guard. In his eulogy, Father Charles O'Donnell, the president of Notre Dame, said, "In this holy week of Christ's passion and death there has occurred a tragic event which accounts for our presence this day. Knute Rockne is dead. And who was he? Ask the president of the United States who dispatched a personal note of tribute; ask the King of Norway; the state legislature; the University Senates; the civic bodies. Ask the Bishops; clergymen; ask the thousands of newspaper men whose labor of love in his memory has stirred a reading public of 125 million Americans.

(top to bottom) Pat O'Brien, pictured with Ronald Reagan, starred in the 1940 film on Rockne's life. ■ A poster advertising Knute Rockne, All American

Ask men and women from every walk of life; ask the children, the boys of America. Yes, ask all of these 'Who was this man whose death has struck the nation with dismay, and everywhere bowed heads in grief?' This was Knute Rockne."

The boy whose first experience playing football left him so bloody and bruised that his parents forbid him to play grew into a man whose contributions remain unparalleled in college football. Even though Knute Rockne became world-renowned for his coaching talent, it was his knack for squeezing the zest out of every facet of life that defined him to his family and close friends. Knute Rockne came to Notre Dame as a chemistry student. By the time he left, he had taught everyone something about the composition of the human spirit.

The Four Horsemen

Just ten days before the Notre Dame–Army game of 1924, a game that ensured the Notre Dame backfield of college football immortality, Knute Rockne confided to a friend that his 1924 team was "anything but good…and our backfield has not got to going yet as a result."

But Rockne's comment wasn't expressing pessimism as much as it was frustration. In their sophomore year, Elmer Layden and Don Miller were starting halfbacks, and Jim Crowley and Harry Stuhldreher were their lead alternates. As juniors in 1923, they had proven themselves a formidable backfield force, even attracting the attention of renowned New York sportswriter Grantland Rice, who characterized them as "a wild horse stampede."

Rice wrote for the *New York Herald-Tribune* and was a member of a category of sportswriters referred to during the time as "Gee-Whizzers," writers prone to using hyperbole to transform mundane sporting events into epics, and athletes into Greek gods. In the pre-television era of the 1920s, fans had limited opportunities to actually see their favorite teams or athletes in person, so they thrived on the mythic descriptions of Rice and his fellow writers.

When Notre Dame came to New York to battle Army on October 18, 1924, the Polo Grounds were filled with fifty-five thousand fans. Among the crowd, watching from the press box, was Grantland Rice:

On the first play the fleet Crowley peeled off fifteen yards and the cloud from the west was now beginning to show signs of lightning and thunder. The fleet, powerful Layden got six yards more and then Don Miller added ten. A forward pass from Stuhldreher to Crowley added twelve yards, and a moment later Don Miller ran twenty yards around Army's right wing….Crowley, Miller and Layden—Miller, Layden and Crowley—one or another, ripping and crashing through, as the Army defense threw everything it had in the way to stop this wild charge that had now come seventy yards. Crowley and Layden added five yards more and then, on a split play, Layden went ten yards across the line as if he had just been fired from the black mouth of a howitzer.

Elmer Layden's touchdown gave Notre Dame a halftime lead of 6 to 0.

During halftime, George Strickler, a Notre Dame student press assistant, was chatting with Rice and other writers in the press box. He was describing a movie he had just seen called *The Four Horsemen of the Apocalypse*, starring Rudolph Valentino. He was especially struck by a cinematic effect that showed the charging ghostly images of Famine, Pestilence, Destruction, and Death. Seeking a lead for his article, Rice was inspired by Strickler's description of the mythic imagery, and began crafting what would

(left to right) The Four Horsemen were immortalized by this photograph arranged by Notre Dame student press assistant George Strickler. The legendary Irish backfield was composed of (left to right) Don Miller (right halfback), Elmer Layden (fullback), Jim Crowley (left halfback), and Harry Stuhldreher (quarterback). ■ Game program from the 1924 Notre Dame–Army game

(clockwise from bottom left) Elmer Layden shows off his kicking skills. ■ Jim Crowley runs with the ball during the 1925 Rose Bowl. ■ The Notre Dame backfield of (left to right) Layden, Crowley, Miller, and Stuhldreher was the subject of much publicity during their final season together.

become the most famous lead line in American sports journalism, and immortalize four Notre Dame backs forever in college football history:

Outlined against a blue-gray October sky, the Four Horsemen rode again. In dramatic lore they are known as Famine, Pestilence, Destruction, and Death. These are only aliases. Their real names are: Stuhldreher, Miller, Crowley and Layden. They formed the crest of the South Bend cyclone before which another fighting Army football team was swept over the precipice at the Polo Grounds yesterday afternoon as 55,000 spectators peered down on the bewildering panorama spread on the green plain below.

In the third quarter, Notre Dame took a 13 to 0 lead on a twenty-yard run and a conversion by Crowley. Army came back with one touchdown in the fourth, but was unable to get past the Irish. The 13 to 7 loss was Army's only defeat for the season.

The remarkable legend of the game began to build the following day. Rice's lead so impressed the *Herald-Tribune* editor that he positioned the account of Notre Dame's victory over the Cadets on the front page of the Sunday edition.

Proud of his unwitting contribution to Rice's creative stroke of genius, Strickler decided to capitalize on the label given to the Notre Dame backs. After the team arrived in South Bend, Strickler arranged to have the players put on their helmets and hop on the backs of the horses, each of them clutching a football. Miller, Layden, Crowley, and Stuhldreher, kids who had no idea how lasting one snapshot would be, posed as the cameras clicked the picture that became the emblem of Notre Dame football in the 1920s and beyond. Only Stuhldreher flashed an obvious smile, but all of the young men enjoyed the attention. "The thing just kind of mushroomed," Crowley said later. National wire services circulated the photo in every major newspaper in America, and the "Four Horsemen" name became as reliable in South Bend as Studebaker.

"After the splurge in the press, the sports fans around the nation, along with other sportswriters, got interested in us," Crowley added. "Our record helped, too. If we'd lost a couple, I don't think we would have been remembered." As a unit, the Four Horsemen played thirty games in four years and lost to only one team, Nebraska, who beat them twice.

In what was their final ride together, the Four Horsemen of the University of Notre Dame made a run for the roses, playing against Stanford in the Rose Bowl on January 1, 1925.

Elmer Layden, the speediest of the four, scored three touchdowns in the 27 to 10 romp over Stanford that afternoon in Pasadena. Two of the scores came on spectacular interception returns of Ernie Nevers passes that jolted Stanford like a Bay Area tremor. The other came when the skinny fullback slithered his way for a three-yard touchdown. Jim Crowley, the crafty halfback whom Curly Lambeau recommended to Notre Dame, kicked three extra points in the game in an era when point-after-touchdowns were anything but routine. Don Miller, once called by Rockne the "greatest open-field runner I've ever seen," added his usual array of jukes to help the Irish control the ball and the clock. Harry Stuhldreher, the quarterback whose brash attitude tested all of coach Knute Rockne's patience, exhibited his toughness and leadership one last time by playing the Rose Bowl with a broken ankle suffered early in the game.

Their last ride together in the Rose Bowl completed a 10–0 season and clinched the national championship. It came as no surprise to anybody associated with the Four Horsemen that their lives after leaving Notre Dame remained stories of success.

Miller, who graduated as Notre Dame's second all-time leading rusher behind only George Gipp, became a lawyer. His distinguished career peaked in 1941 when President Franklin Roosevelt appointed Miller U.S. District Attorney.

Stuhldreher, whose first taste of football growing up in Ohio came from watching Knute Rockne play pro football for the Massillon Tigers, applied his leadership skills to the coaching profession. After a stint as head coach at Villanova, he became the University of Wisconsin's athletic director and football coach. After leaving the game he loved, Stuhldreher became an executive at U.S. Steel in Pittsburgh and wrote two books.

Crowley also became a successful coach. He led Michigan State for four years before taking over at Fordham University, where he coached Vince

Lombardi. Crowley later joined the U.S. Navy, became the first commissioner of the All-America Football Conference, dabbled in broadcasting, and showed as much versatility in business as he did in the backfield.

Layden got his law degree, but instead went into coaching. A 48–16–6 record at Duquesne University in Pittsburgh piqued the interest of his alma mater, who brought him back to coach the Irish in 1934. Over seven years, Layden's teams went 47–13–3. He was considered a solid coach, but not so legendary that he ever outgrew the label, "former Four Horseman of Notre Dame." Of course, that designation never bothered Layden anyway.

Miller, Layden, Crowley, and Stuhldreher. None of them stood taller than 6 feet, and none weighed more than 162 pounds. But their collective dominance in the backfield, underscored by the words of Grantland Rice, placed the Four Horsemen among the giants in college football history.

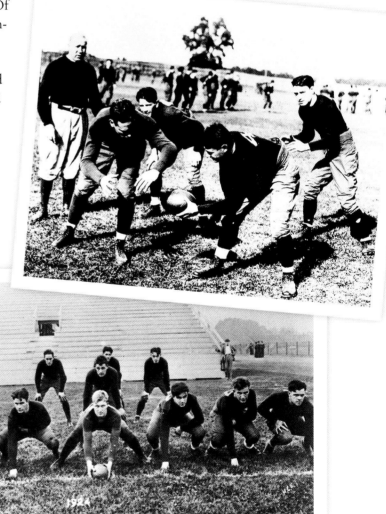

(top to bottom) Rockne (left) looks on as (from left) Miller, Layden, Stuhldreher, and Crowley practice a play. ■ The Notre Dame offense—with the "Seven Mules" blocking for the Four Horsemen—in 1924

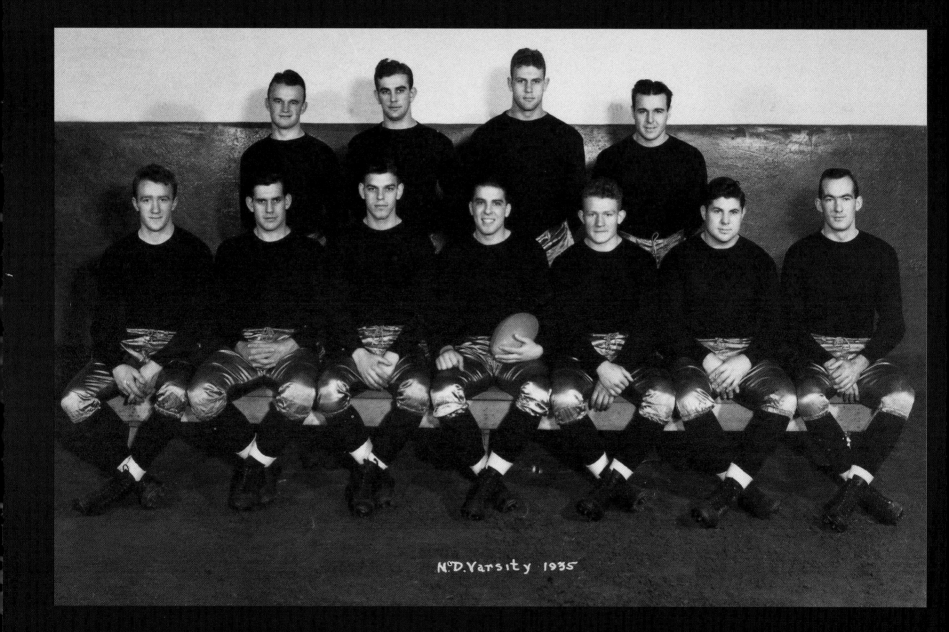

N. D. Varsity 1935

The Original "Game of the Century"

Andy Pilney was not performing up to the high standards Notre Dame head football coach Elmer Layden had set for his talented senior running back. So, with a dream matchup with undefeated Ohio State upcoming, Layden, the former Notre Dame back of Four Horsemen fame, turned to a psychological ploy perfected by his coaching mentor, Knute Rockne.

Rockne often used the media to light a fire under his players. In the 1920s, the *South Bend Tribune* published a column known as "Bearskin," ghostwritten by Rockne. He used the alias to criticize his players, keeping them from getting a cocky attitude. Layden called on Notre Dame Sports Information Director Joe Petritz to help him revive the "Bearskin" column just before the Ohio State game. In the article, Layden brought Pilney back to Earth, calling him on the carpet for a fumbling problem.

The Fighting Irish had another intangible inspiring them as well. The March prior to the 1935 season, captain-elect and starting tackle Joe Sullivan died of pneumonia. "We said a prayer for Joe prior to every game," said Pilney. "Everyone looked up to him and his memory helped us carry through the season." Layden needed every ploy in his arsenal if the Irish were to topple Ohio State on its home turf, a feat most would consider an upset.

Notre Dame was also undefeated, 5–0, heading into the game at Ohio Stadium on Saturday, November 2, 1935. Nonetheless, most prognosticators made Ohio State the favorite. Notre Dame had barely escaped with a couple of close wins earlier in the season, including a 9 to 6 victory over Pittsburgh. Marty Peters booted a field goal to win that game in the final seconds, but many Pittsburgh players and fans believed the kick had actually gone wide.

The hype for the Notre Dame vs. Ohio State game might have brought about the weekly Associated Press poll, which started the following season. Had there been polls in 1935, this might have been a No. 1 vs. No. 2 matchup. The media list covering the contest was a who's-who of the era, indicating that the scribes considered it a battle of heavyweights. Grantland Rice, Damon Runyon, and Paul Gallico described it for their major newspapers, and Bill Stern and Red Barber were all on hand to call the game on national radio. Tickets were being scalped for as much as $50. Eighty-one thousand packed into the Horseshoe—one of the largest crowds ever at Ohio State—causing this game to be considered the first college football game heralded as the "Game of the Century."

The first half seemed to verify the pregame predictions. The Buckeyes of head coach Francis Schmidt dominated the Irish. Using a power running

(left to right) 1935 varsity team photo of the Fighting Irish ■ *Game program and ticket from the "Game of the Century"*

(top to bottom) A view of Ohio Stadium in 1935 ■ Action on the field in the 1935 game

game featuring laterals and quick pitches, Notre Dame spent the first half grasping at air. The Buckeyes scored a pair of touchdowns to take a 13 to 0 lead. But Layden did not take out his frustrations with a tirade in his halftime talk. He later wrote, "I felt my team needed settling down, not pepping up. We had bad breaks in the first half and made some mistakes. As calmly as possible, I tried to discuss what we hadn't done right and should correct in the thirty minutes we had left."

Layden did make one major change. Going into the third period, he started his second unit, featuring Pilney at left halfback. The change did not lead to immediate success in the scoring column, but the fresh second team stole the momentum from the larger Ohio State players.

Finally, on the final play of the third period, and still trailing 13 to 0, Pilney returned an Ohio State punt forty-seven yards to the Buckeye thirteen. A twelve-yard pass from Pilney to Frank Gaul set up Notre Dame's first score, a two-yard run by Steve Miller. But Ken Stilley missed the conversion.

Notre Dame shut down Ohio State offensively on the next possession, then launched a furious drive to the Buckeyes' one-yard line. Again, Miller drove for the goal line, but, as he landed in the end zone, he fumbled

the ball and Ohio State recovered. "In those days you had to come down in the end zone with possession," recalled Chet Grant, Notre Dame's backfield coach at the time. "Miller broke the plane, it would have been a touchdown today, but not in 1935."

Notre Dame's defense bent but did not break, giving Pilney and the Irish offense the ball back at their own twenty. Pilney connected on two passes in a drive that set up a thirty-three–yard touchdown pass to Mike Layden, the brother of the Notre Dame head coach. There were just two minutes left in the game and the Irish could tie it with a successful conversion. But, this time, Wally Fromhart's kick hit the crossbar and bounced away. The Irish attempted an onside kick on the ensuing kickoff, but the Buckeyes recovered, apparently ending Notre Dame's incredible come-back. Ohio State only had to run down the clock.

The Buckeyes called for an end-run, with Dick Beltz carrying the ball on an apparent game-ending ground attack. Pilney, at this point in the game playing defense, hit Beltz in the midsection, jarring the ball loose. The pigskin rolled toward the sideline, but Irish center Hank Pojman touched the ball before it went out of bounds, giving Notre Dame possession. Today's rules would have allowed Ohio State to retain possession, but in 1935, the last team to touch a fumble before it went out of bounds gained control.

Notre Dame now had the ball at the Ohio State forty-nine with a minute left. Pilney had one last heroic play

in him. It was a run that wide receiver Wayne Millner recalled vividly.

"Pilney faked a pass," said Millner, "raced through a hole at center, dodged eight separate Ohio State men, and finally was pinned at the nineteen-yard line by the three remaining Buckeyes." Pilney suffered a severe knee injury on the play and left the field on a stretcher. It was his last play as a Notre Dame football player. It was a fourth-period performance of legendary proportions. Pilney had five rushes for forty-five yards and connected on five of six passes for 121 yards, not to mention his tackle that caused the fumble, giving Notre Dame the ball for one final opportunity.

With Pilney out of the game, Layden sent Bill Shakespeare into the contest. Shakespeare finished third in the first-ever Heisman Trophy balloting in 1935, but had been on the bench most of the second half. After a couple of plays led to no yardage, Layden needed to send in another play, but substitution rules of the era forced him to turn to fourth-team quarterback Jim McKenna, a player who wasn't even supposed to be at the game. McKenna had suffered an injury in practice the week of the game and had not been named to the travel squad. But he desperately wanted to attend the game, so he snuck on the team train and hid in a teammate's berth.

McKenna called the signals and took the snap. Shakespeare faded back. McKenna handed him the ball, and then executed a perfect block on Ohio State's Charles Hamrick, who was thirty pounds heavier. Avoiding the rush, Shakespeare heaved the ball to the end zone to the waiting arms of Millner, giving the Irish an improbable 18 to 13 lead. It was one of just nineteen completions for Shakespeare all season. For the third straight score, Notre Dame missed the extra point, but with just a few left, it was inconsequential. Ohio State's final play failed and Notre Dame fans from coast to coast celebrated their team's remarkable victory.

While Irish fans rejoiced, Ohio State fans sat stunned for nearly fifteen minutes after the gun sounded. In the joyous postgame locker room, Pilney, who had passed out on his stretcher ride to the locker room, finally regained consciousness. Alongside him was a distinguished man wearing a gray Stetson hat and holding a pad of paper and a pen. "Andy, I've been writing and watching football for over forty years now, and that is the greatest single performance I've ever seen." That was no "Bearskin" account of the game. It was the highly regarded impression of the renowned sportswriter, Grantland Rice, who nearly a dozen years before had immortalized Layden and his Four Horsemen teammates.

(top to bottom) Notre Dame and Ohio State battle on the ground.
■ *Players dive for a loose ball.*

A Heisman History

Each year, the Heisman Trophy is awarded to college football's most exceptional player. The Notre Dame Fighting Irish were forever linked to the coveted award when Jim Crowley, one of Notre Dame's famous Four Horsemen, helped design the bronze trophy sculpted by Frank Eliscu. But over the years, Irish players haven't allowed the connection to stop there. Of the winners since the Heisman was first handed out in 1935, a record seven Fighting Irish players have been recognized with this most prestigious collegiate award. But as great as these trophy winners became, each had his own unique challenges to overcome on his way to college football's pinnacle.

Angelo Bertelli won Notre Dame's first Heisman Trophy in 1943 despite playing in only six games for the Irish that year. Bertelli's season ended early when he left Notre Dame to join the war effort with the Marines. He later admitted that his Heisman was probably the voters rewarding him for great seasons in 1941 and 1942, as much as it was for his six games in 1943. Still, he demonstrated remarkable abilities in those six games, against formidable opponents including third-ranked Navy and second-ranked Michigan. Bertelli completed five of eight passes for two touchdowns, leading the Irish to a 35 to 12 victory over Michigan in front of a stunned capacity crowd in Ann Arbor.

In the six games, he threw for 511 yards, ten touchdown passes, and posted a 69.4 percent completion rate. The success of the 1943 team was also attributable in part to coach Frank Leahy's scrapping the traditional Rockne-era "Box Formation" offense and implementing the new T-formation the year before.

NOTRE DAME'S HEISMAN WINNERS
∎

Angelo Bertelli, *1943*

Johnny Lujack, *1947*

Leon Hart, *1949*

Johnny Lattner, *1953*

Paul Hornung, *1956*

John Huarte, *1964*

Tim Brown, *1987*

Father Theodore M. Hesburgh, C.S.C., and Rev. Edmund P. Joyce, C.S.C., pose with Notre Dame's Heisman winners. (left to right): Lujack, Bertelli, Hart, Brown, Hornung, Huarte, and Lattner.
∎ *Angelo Bertelli in a posed kicking shot*

Bertelli carries the ball for a long gain against Arizona.

athlete who earned varsity monograms in basketball, track and field, and baseball. The youngest of four sons in a blue-collar Polish family, Lujack said, "Sports was our main recreation because we didn't have any money to do other things."

Lujack is the first athlete in Notre Dame's history to letter in four different sports in his first year of eligibility. However, in Lujack's football debut in 1943, he went the wrong way on a play and was handily clobbered. After he did it a second time, he jogged over to the sidelines where Coach Frank Leahy asked how he felt. "My head hurts," Lujack admitted to his coach. Leahy quickly answered, "I don't know why. You haven't been using it." But Lujack rebounded from that inauspicious start to fill Bertelli's shoes.

Unlike the hoopla surrounding today's Heisman presentations, Bertelli found out about his honor when he was handed a telegram just after he had exited a Quonset hut on Parris Island where he was going through boot camp. It was a bittersweet moment for Bertelli. He had to wipe away tears, not of joy but of sorrow. He had just listened to unranked Great Lakes upset Notre Dame, 19 to 14, to cost his team a perfect season. "I left the room crying and when I went outside, that's when I was handed the telegram that I had won the Heisman," the Massachusetts native said.

While World War II ended Bertelli's Irish career, it only interrupted Lujack's. He left for the service later in 1943. His three years of active duty included several months on a submarine chaser in the English Channel. He credits those years with helping him mature and develop physically. "I felt very fortunate that I was able to return in better shape and not injured," he said. When he returned in 1946, it didn't take long to regain his form on the football field.

Bertelli's replacement at quarterback on that 1943 team was none other than Johnny Lujack, a sophomore from Connelsville, Pennsylvania, a town of seventeen thousand nestled in the western Allegheny mountains, home of another future Irish quarterback, Joe Montana. At first blush, it appeared that Lujack had a long way to go to match up to Bertelli. Lujack was an all-around

Perhaps nothing reflects the conviction of Lujack's return like his individual efforts on a single play at Yankee Stadium against Army on November 9, 1946. Entering the game against the No. 2 Irish, No. 1 Army was riding a twenty-five game winning streak and well on their way to a third consecutive national championship. Media hype and build-up for the game was at an all-time high. With the score tied at zero in the third quarter, and neither team making much headway against the other, Army's 1945 Heisman Trophy winner, Doc Blanchard, broke free for what would have been the winning touchdown, with just one man to beat. Fortunately for the Irish, that man was Johnny Lujack.

Despite playing with a sprained ankle, Lujack caught Blanchard and took him down at the Notre Dame thirty-seven–yard line with a game-saving, shoestring tackle. The game ended in a 0 to 0 tie, and Notre Dame finished the season as undefeated national champions.

The *Boston Herald* proclaimed Lujack's 1947 Irish team "the greatest Notre Dame squad of all time. Its third string could whip most varsities." Their 9–0 record was the first perfect season in seventeen years. In their first game of the season against Pittsburgh, the Irish suffered six turnovers, but

(left to right) Quarterback Johnny Lujack poses for a publicity photo. ■ Lujack scores on a thirty-one–yard sweep.

Lujack led Notre Dame back to win 40 to 6. Northwestern came the closest of any team to beating Notre Dame that year, but the Irish won 26 to 19.

For his career, and on his way to winning the 1947 Heisman, Lujack passed for 2,080 yards, threw nineteen touchdown passes, ran for 438 yards, and scored another two touchdowns on the ground. Lujack went onto to play in the burgeoning NFL with the Chicago Bears.

(left to right) End Leon Hart strikes a pose in 1949. ■ Hart catches a pass from quarterback Johnny Lujack against Army in 1947.

One of the players on the receiving end of Lujack's passes for the Irish was Leon Hart, the 1949 Heisman Trophy winner. Leon Hart also stumbled, quite literally, out of the blocks to start his college football career. When the freshman Hart, from Turtle Creek, Pennsylvania, dashed onto the field for his first playing action in

1946, he looked over his shoulder to hear what an assistant coach was yelling and accidentally ran over teammate Bob Livingstone.

In fact, Hart was just happy to make the team after the veterans returned from the war his freshman year. "When I got to Notre Dame, there were twenty-one ends; thirteen of them letter winners," he said. "You had to learn quickly to survive." Hart's slow start didn't seem to slow down the Irish though. Incredibly, Notre Dame did not lose a single game during his entire four-year career, going 36–0–2 and winning three national championships.

Hart played both offense and defense for the Irish, amassing in his career 112 yards and two touchdowns rushing, 751 yards and twelve touchdowns receiving, one blocked kick, and eight fumble recoveries. In the final game of the 1949 season, Notre Dame expected to easily roll over Southern Methodist University. But despite being without its top player, 1948 Heisman winner Doak Walker, SMU surprised the Irish and threatened Notre Dame's four-year unbeaten streak. With little more than nine minutes left in the game, the score was tied at 20. Leon Hart moved from linebacker to

fullback, powering for fifty-four crucial yards as Notre Dame drove to a touchdown, putting the Irish in the lead 27 to 20. But the Mustangs still had time to score. Hart showed what Heisman winners were made of by rousing the Notre Dame defense and holding SMU on the Notre Dame one-foot line. In the final play of the game, Notre Dame's Jerry Groom intercepted a Kyle Rote pass that would have given SMU a tying touchdown, icing the victory, and leaving the Notre Dame streak intact. To this day, Leon Hart remains one of only two linemen in history to take home the Heisman.

Johnny Lattner won the Heisman Trophy in 1953 during his senior year, despite the fact that he didn't lead the Irish in rushing, passing, receiving, or scoring. He did play both offense and defense. Lattner, too, overcame a dismal start to eventually win his Heisman. As a junior in 1952, he fumbled the ball five times against Purdue. He was told by Leahy, "I want you to go to the chapel and confess the five mortal sins you committed against the enemy on Saturday." Without a doubt, Lattner would redeem himself in the 1953 season.

Going into the Oklahoma game in 1953, Lattner was questionable to start because of a sprained ankle. Leahy only started him because backfield coach Bill Earley insisted that Lattner should "because he's an All-American." When Lattner dribbled the opening kickoff out of bounds, Leahy turned to Earley and said, "There is *your* All-American."

But in the final two minutes of the contest, Notre Dame was ahead by seven. It was second down and ten for Oklahoma on the Notre Dame

forty-four–yard line. Lattner, who had led the Irish the year before in pass interceptions, jumped high into the air, intercepted the pass on the thirty-yard line, and ran it back to the thirty-three–yard line, before taking a jarring tackle from the Sooners' Melvin Brown. With just a 1:48 left in the game, Notre Dame simply ran the clock down to a 28 to 21 victory. That's when Bill Earley yelled back at Leahy, "Yes, Coach, *there* is your All-American."

The kid from Chicago became Notre Dame's fourth Heisman Trophy winner. For his career, Lattner set the school record for all-purpose yards (3,250 total yards). He also averaged forty-four yards on kickoff returns, picked off thirteen enemy passes, and recovered eight fumbles. Lattner went on to play one year in the NFL with the Pittsburgh Steelers, but later suffered a career-ending knee injury in a military game.

(left to right) Lattner in a posed kicking shot ■ *Halfback Johnny Lattner in an action pose in 1953*

HORNUNG

In 1956, twenty-one–year old Paul Hornung of Louisville, Kentucky, broke Lattner's all-purpose yards record with an individual performance that may never be equaled. In fact, Hornung, known as "the Irish golden boy," partly because of his looks and partly because of his clutch play, played quarterback, left halfback, fullback, and safety, and remains the only player from a losing team (Notre Dame finished 2–8 in 1956) ever to win the Heisman Trophy.

Hornung averaged 6.1 points per game as the backup fullback in his sophomore year. He racked up 1,215 yards in total offense his junior year, placing fourth nationally, and fifth in that year's Heisman voting. Playing with one dislocated thumb through much of the season, and two of them by the end, Hornung had a tremendous 1956 season anyway.

On October 6, 1956, in the second game of the season, Notre Dame played host to Indiana. Once again, Hornung was a one-man show, even serving as kicker. Notre Dame was fourth and seven on the Indiana eleven when Hornung capped a precise fifty-three–yard, eight-play drive with a perfect touchdown pass to Aubrey Lewis. The Irish beat Indiana 20 to 6.

He passed and ran for 354 yards, setting an NCAA record in a loss to USC that year. He ranked second nationally in total offense (1,337 yards) and led the Irish in rushing, passing, return yardage, scoring, and minutes played. "That season, we basically had one play," recalls Ed Sullivan, Hornung's center on the team. "I'd hike the ball to Paul, and we'd all just get the hell out of the way!"

(left to right) Notre Dame quarterback Paul Hornung running a "keeper" play against Iowa in 1955 ■ In 1956, Paul Hornung became the third Irish quarterback to win the trophy.

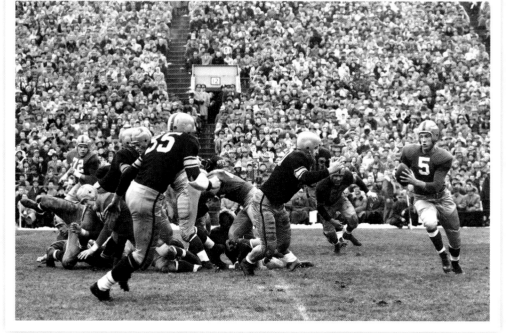

HUARTE

Never in the history of the Heisman was there a more surprising success story than that of Irish quarterback John Huarte in 1964. His rise to the top of his sport is the stuff of legend. Huarte did not play as a freshman. As a sophomore, he was injured much of the year. As a junior and third-string quarterback on a 2–7 team, Huarte didn't play enough to earn a letter. Even so, first-year Notre Dame coach Ara Parseghian saw something in him that he liked in the spring of 1964.

Just before Huarte could play in the spring game, however, he partially separated his shoulder during a scrimmage. Huarte was scheduled to undergo a surgery that would have ended his college career. But at the last minute, Parseghian decided to send him to Chicago for a second opinion. It actually took a third opinion, and then a fourth opinion, before rest instead of surgery was prescribed. Huarte bounced back in the fall of 1964 to have a sensational season, setting twelve school records in passing, reviving a Notre Dame football program that had been floundering for the five seasons prior, and winning the Heisman.

Notre Dame quarterback John Huarte runs with the ball and leaps past Michigan State defenders on his way to a fourth-quarter touchdown.

In Notre Dame's 1964 season opener against Wisconsin, Huarte found teammate Jack Snow, who himself finished fifth in the voting that year, on touchdown throws of sixty-one and forty-two yards. With a Huarte-to-Snow combination that would shine throughout the year, the Irish were off to the races. A California native, Huarte led the Irish to the No. 1 ranking and a 9–0 record before USC rebounded from a 17 to 0 halftime deficit to defeat Notre Dame on a heartbreaking touchdown with 1:33 to play. The national championship got away from the Irish, but Huarte still captured the Heisman. In that single season, Huarte passed for an incredible 2,062 yards and sixteen touchdowns.

(left to right) Huarte was the sixth Irish player to receive the Heisman. ■ Huarte pictured with his Heisman Trophy in 1964

BROWN

It would be twenty-three more years before another Irish player won the heralded trophy. The player who broke the drought was Tim Brown in 1987. Before winning the Heisman, however, Brown also persevered an infamous beginning much like several of his Fighting Irish Heisman-winning predecessors. When Brown touched the football for Notre Dame for the first time, it was only for a brief moment. He was trying to field the first kickoff of the 1984 season in the inaugural football game at the Hoosier Dome in Indianapolis against Purdue. The kickoff bounced off his chest, dribbled between his legs, eluded his desperate grasp, and was recovered by a Purdue defender. The Boilermakers went on to kick a field goal after the fumble and eventually beat the Irish by two points, 23 to 21. Tim Brown thought that first college play might be his last. "I wanted to go home after that," he later admitted. When the lightning-fast Irish wide receiver finally did go home to Dallas, Texas, at the end of his collegiate career, he was playing in the 1988 Cotton Bowl and had been named Notre Dame's seventh Heisman Trophy winner.

Tim Brown in action against Michigan in 1987

(left to right) Brown in action in 1987 ■ Brown accepts his trophy from Eugene Meyer.

Most would agree that Tim Brown won the 1987 Heisman long before the official ceremony in December. To be exact, it was Saturday, September 17, 1987, at a night game against Michigan State. Brown had already drawn national attention the year before with a dramatic, year-ending, fifty-six–yard punt return against USC to set up a game-winning field goal with no time left on the clock. In the 1987 season opener against Michigan, Brown catapulted himself above several defenders to make a nearly impossible catch that set the tone for an Irish victory over the No. 9 Wolverines. But it was a week later against the Michigan State Spartans that lightning would strike twice and Tim Brown would all but be crowned the Heisman Trophy winner.

With Notre Dame up 5 to 0 in the first quarter and the Irish defense forcing the Spartans to punt on fourth and seventeen, Brown fielded the punt at his own twenty-nine–yard line. He turned upfield, cut toward the far sideline, then sprinted to the end zone. Now with a 12 to 0 lead, and still in the first quarter, the Spartans were once more forced to punt. Again, Brown fielded the ball deep in his own terri-tory and took off. After breaking several tackles, he had only the punter to beat. Brown cut, faked, and turned upfield. The Spartan punter was left pret-zeled on the ground as Brown crossed the goal line.

By the end of the first quarter, Brown had almost single-handedly beaten that year's eventual Big

Ten and Rose Bowl champion Spartans. In the first half of the game alone, he had 231 all-purpose yards. Brown's career statistics were similarly astonishing. While at Notre Dame, Brown ran for 442 yards and four touchdowns, had 2,493 receiving yards and fourteen touchdown receptions, returned kickoffs for 1,613 yards and three touchdowns, and returned punts for 476 yards and three more touchdowns.

Besides the seven Heisman Trophy winners, the Fighting Irish have had three runners-up, five third-place finishers, four fourth-place finishers, and seven who finished fifth. In the years the trophy has been awarded, at least one Notre Dame player has placed in the top ten in thirty-three of those seasons. Some Fighting Irish whose quest for the Heisman ended just short of the top were Bill Shakespeare in 1935, Johnny Lujack in 1946, Nick Eddy in 1966, Terry Hanratty in 1968, and Ken McAfee in 1977. All finished third in the voting. Joe Theismann, whose last name pronunciation was changed to rhyme with Heisman, finished second to Stanford's Jim Plunkett in 1970. Bertelli, too, was a second-place finisher in 1941. But the closest the Irish had to an eighth recipient was in 1990 when Raghib "Rocket" Ismail finished second, to the surprise of many, to Brigham Young quarterback Ty Detmer.

Today, the Heisman Trophy remains the most recognizable, prestigious award offered in collegiate sports, and Notre Dame's place in its rich history is unequaled. Bertelli, Lujack, Hart, Lattner, Hornung, Huarte, and Brown. As they have for over a century, Notre Dame players will figure into the Heisman equation. And, whether in triumph or challenge, they will continue to shine like the dome under which they play. So if that freshman should fumble a punt or that sophomore quarterback happens to stumble out of the huddle, don't be too quick to judge. You just might be watching Notre Dame's eighth Heisman Trophy winner, and the beginning of a historic career.

The Eighth Heisman Trophy for Notre Dame?

To this day, Irish fans claim that the best college football player of 1990 was mistakenly passed over in the Heisman voting. Vindication would come almost immediately, as Ty Detmer followed his acceptance of the Heisman Trophy with a four-interception performance in a Brigham Young loss to Hawaii. Ismail, on the other hand, reaffirmed his claim to the honor with a stellar performance against No. 1–ranked Colorado in the 1991 Orange Bowl. Ismail came close to single-handedly upsetting the national champions that New Year's Day.

With the Irish down by a single point and victory only a minute away for Colorado, the Irish defense shut down the Buffaloes one last time, forcing them to punt with forty-three seconds left in the game. No one, including the television network announcers, imagined that Colorado would actually kick the ball to Ismail. With a simple punt out-of-bounds and a stop or two by the Colorado defense, the national championship was theirs. To the surprise of all, Colorado did kick to Ismail.

Ismail grabbed the ball at his own nine-yard line and burst upfield with no intention of stopping until he scored. The fastest man in Notre Dame football history went untouched the entire ninety-one yards. For a moment, Notre Dame had experienced yet another gridiron miracle. Unfortunately, what would have been a game-winning, last-second punt return for a touchdown was called back as a result of a late clipping penalty. The Irish did not have another miracle in their bag to come back in those final seconds. They lost 10 to 9.

Whether the touchdown should have counted or not, those who witnessed it agree, the Rocket's grand finale was truly a Heisman-worthy performance.

Notre Dame Ends Oklahoma Winning Streak

As a three-touchdown underdog, no one expected much from Notre Dame in their 1957 showdown with Oklahoma. A year earlier, coach Bud Wilkinson's Oklahoma Sooners had thrashed the Irish 40 to 0 in South Bend. Notre Dame ended the '56 season with a record of 2–8, one of the worst in their history. Now, coming into their showdown in Norman, on November 15, 1957, Wilkinson's winning streak stood at an astonishing forty-seven games, a collegiate record. Oklahoma was also gunning for its third consecutive national championship.

Naturally, the game attracted a sellout crowd. Moreover, the contest was carried live on national television, on NBC. As for poetic symmetry, the last team to defeat Oklahoma before the Sooners went on their incredible victory march was Notre Dame in 1953.

It was the perfect setup.

"The wind was blowing red dust through this little town outside Norman, where we stayed," Notre Dame's Monty Stickles recalled. "When we went to Mass that morning, a group of young children—eight, nine, ten years old—were waiting outside the church with their parents. They were begging us to win so they could have bragging rights against the Baptists. It was kind of a 'win one for the Catholics' thing."

The Irish rolled into Norman with a record of 4–2. Having been pummeled by Oklahoma a year earlier, Irish coach Brennan knew the Sooners were big, fast, and bruising. But Oklahoma's very dominance of the college game made them susceptible to the hubris of predictability, a hidden weakness Brennan looked to exploit.

"When you have great success as Oklahoma did, there's a tendency to keep on doing what you're doing," Brennan said. "They were running five plays

(left to right) Halfback Dick Lynch receives a pitchout from quarterback Bobby Williams and races three yards for the game's only score. ■ Sooner faithful prepare for another Oklahoma victory. ■ November 16, 1957, game program and ticket

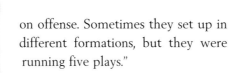

on offense. Sometimes they set up in different formations, but they were running five plays."

Not believing his defense could dominate Oklahoma head-to-head, Brennan employed a new defensive strategy. His defensive linemen attacked the gaps in the Sooners offensive line and tried to penetrate the backfield. So risky was the move that Brennan insisted on calling the defensive sets himself that day. The strategy was chancy but proved effective. The score at halftime was 0–0.

In the end it came down to four plays from the Oklahoma eight-yard line, where the Sooners defense had proved impenetrable earlier in the game. Pietrosante surged up the middle for four. Williams advanced it one on a keeper. Lynch was stopped for no gain.

Now, it was fourth and goal-to-go from the three. The Sooners put eight men on their defensive line and pulled their three linebackers up near the line of scrimmage. "They were in tight, looking for an off-tackle slant," Brennan said. They were looking for Pietrosante.

Williams crossed them up. "Bobby had them guessing," Lynch recalls. "He called a fake off-tackle to Nick and a pitch out to me, and it was wide open. It was a great fake by Bobby. I ran around the right side and it was wide open for a touchdown."

(left to right) Sooner star Jackie Sandefer is hauled down by a Notre Dame tackler. ■ Jubilant Irish players join students in carrying coach Terry Brennan off the field after Notre Dame beat the "unbeatable" Oklahoma Sooners.

(opposite page, left to right) News of the Irish upset dominated the front page of the next morning's South Bend Tribune. *■ Action from the 1952 Oklahoma–Notre Dame game*

The turning point finally came in the fourth quarter. Starting from his own twenty-yard line, Notre Dame quarterback Bobby Williams called every play on a punishing drive. He handed off to fullback Nick Pietrosante, a star for the ages who seasoned his own legend by battering his way downfield with a ferocity that more than one observer described as "savage." Halfback Dick Lynch took the ball and rammed it up inside the tackles. Williams hit Dick Royer with a ten-yard jump pass for another first down at the Sooners nineteen-yard line.

Stickles booted the extra point to make it 7 to 0 with just under four minutes to play. Oklahoma's desperate attempt to hold onto its streak ended when Williams intercepted a pass into the end zone in the final play of the game. The Irish had not only broken the mighty Sooners streak, they handed them their first shutout in 123 games. Irish cocaptain Ed Sullivan observed that Sooner fans were so stunned they didn't begin to move from their seats for nearly twenty minutes after the game. "I thought to myself, 'this is what Notre Dame football is all about'" Sullivan recalls.

The Hit Heard 'Round the World

November 8, 1952

It was a matchup that turned out to be one of the greatest games in Notre Dame history. But it was a bone-crushing defensive play in the fourth quarter, dubbed "the hit heard 'round the world," that placed the game in Notre Dame lore.

The Oklahoma Sooners visited South Bend as a thirteen-point favorite. Oklahoma's Billy Vessels, who would win the Heisman Trophy that season, ran roughshod through Notre Dame, amassing 195 yards. But the Irish defense forced six turnovers and kept it close.

After the Irish tied the game at twenty-one at the outset of the fourth quarter, the biggest play of the contest was about to make the ground quake. On the ensuing kickoff, Oklahoma's Larry Grigg fielded the ball on the two-yard line before heading upfield. With a crashing force at the Oklahoma twenty-four, he ran head-on into Irish linebacker Dan Shannon. The collision was brutal.

"It was like two freight trains coming together," Irish star John Lattner said. Longtime South Bend Tribune sports editor Joe Doyle recalls, "You could actually hear that tackle up in the press box." Grigg and Shannon, however, only heard bells. Each fell backward as the ball popped free and Notre Dame fell on it at the Sooners nineteen. The stands erupted with a cheer as thunderous as the hit itself. Shannon and Grigg were helped off the field. The Irish scored three plays later on Tom Carey's quarterback sneak, and then held on to complete the upset, 27 to 21.

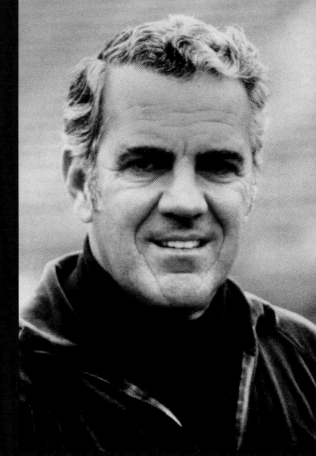

The Great Irish Coaches

They were four Notre Dame men, yet each his own man. They were separated by age and eras, by innovation and renovation, and yet they were united by the same strength, the same indomitable spirit.

Frank Leahy used to drive his players so hard in practice that they would drop to the ground and gasp for breath, only to be told to get back up and run the play again. He believed "perfection is the residue of hard work," and by the time his players graduated, they believed it too.

Ara Parseghian practiced his players in much the same way. If his players got tired enough to keel over in exhaustion, fine, Ara would jump into the blocking drill himself.

Lou Holtz once broke a finger trying to catch a punt after yelling a player off the field. He stopped fielding punts, but he never stopped pacing around practice, prowling from drill to drill.

Dan Devine may have been more hands-off, but that didn't mean he approached the Notre Dame head coaching job any less head-on. Devine understood what many in the position have not, that Notre Dame coaches cannot tiptoe, cannot waver, cannot test the waters. He must be swift and decisive, but mostly resolute, traits that each of these four coaches had in common with the one man

whose shadow they would always stand in—Knute Rockne.

They were strong and focused, and no matter how much public opinion swirled around them, no matter how heavy the burden of expectation piled on their shoulders, their wills remained unbent.

Leahy bucked tradition by changing the offense from the "Box Formation" to the T-formation in 1943, causing a stir, but winning a national championship. Parseghian had to withstand the critics who questioned his decision to settle for a 10 to 10 tie against Michigan State in 1966, but stayed the course that eventually took the Irish to another national title. Devine had to listen to his share of grumbling that quickly quieted when he turned to Joe Montana, a little-known, often lethargic practice player, to bail out the 1977 season. And Holtz, who it seemed encountered controversy around every corner, needed every ounce of fortitude in his slight frame to withstand the scrutiny the modern media and fan base directed his way every season.

Each of these men changed the temperature of a room when they walked into it, not to mention the climate of the Notre Dame football program.

NOTRE DAME'S WINNINGEST COACHES

■

Coach	Years	Record
Knute Rockne	1918–1930	105–12–5
Lou Holtz	1986–1996	100–30–2
Ara Parseghian	1964–1974	95–17–4
Frank Leahy	1941–1943 1946–1953	87–11–9
Dan Devine	1975–1980	53–16–1
Elmer Layden	1934–1940	47–13–3
Jesse Harper	1913–1917	34–5–1

(opposite page, clockwise from top left)
Leahy, Parseghian, Devine, and Holtz

(top to bottom) An intense Leahy watches his team from the sidelines. ■ Leahy instructs his players on the sidelines during his first game as Irish coach.

Leahy simply refused to settle for anything less than excellence, Parseghian did the work of two men, Devine used unpredictability to his advantage, while Holtz spun his oratorical web effectively enough to restore the aura. Each of them, in his own unique way, gave fans ample reason to believe in their invincibility. Yet each of them, ironically, moved out of the most coveted office in college football when it was proven that they were indeed vulnerable.

National titles and an undaunted commitment will always link their careers in Notre Dame lore, and medical history will always connect their exits. Every one of these Notre Dame coaching legends put a period on their Irish coaching tenure because of health problems involving himself or his family. It was the best coaching job in America, yes. But it also could be the most unrelenting, unwieldy, and unforgiving.

Leahy should have known how grueling the job could be. It was sharing a hospital room with Rockne at the Mayo Clinic in Rochester, Minnesota, after the 1930 season that Leahy began thinking of a coaching career. Rockne had checked himself in to take care of phlebitis and asked Leahy to come along to get his injured knee checked out. In their week together, Rockne filled Leahy's ears with the directions that would later help him assemble a Notre Dame dynasty. "In the week I was confined to a hospital bed, I learned more about football and the technique of coaching than in all my previous college playing," Leahy later said. "Right then I decided to become a head coach." Not just any head coach, but just maybe the head coach who gave Notre Dame its national distinction in post–World War II America.

Leahy took over for Elmer Layden in 1941 and immediately instilled the same hard-charging style that he used to go 20–2 at Boston College before coming to Notre Dame. He was smart, he was demanding, and the players he affectionately called his "lads," went 8–0–1 in his first season.

But it wasn't until 1946, perhaps, when the Notre Dame dynasty once again took shape. Leahy had just returned to his job under the Golden Dome after serving two years in the U.S. Navy during World War II. He expected his players to respond like the soldiers he had come to know and even instituted a platoon system that kept his team fresh and ready. America was starving for a success story that had nothing to do with tanks and gunfire, and South Bend was hungry for another national title. Leahy's unbeaten 1946 team fit the bill. His teams never let up for the rest of the decade, going 36–0–2 from the end of the war until the end of the 1949 season. That included two consensus national titles in '47 and '49.

As a result, Notre Dame became a brand name for excellence across America, the Golden Dome an enduring symbol of success. The pressure to meet those lofty expectations finally got to Leahy while he was still a young man. Just forty-five in 1953, he collapsed at halftime of the Georgia Tech game because of an inflamed pancreas. He retired at the end of the year with an astounding 87–11–9 record in eleven years, including six unbeaten seasons, four consensus national titles, and a thirty-nine–game unbeaten streak. "Be a fighter, gents," Leahy often told his team, "not only out there on the football field, but out in life as well."

After Leahy left South Bend in 1954, the Notre Dame program experienced a decade in relative decline. The Irish went just 49–41 in that span, and the echoes had begun to quiet. A new Ara changed all that.

Ara Parseghian had been a fan of Notre Dame football since childhood. "Will become the coach of Notre Dame" was the prediction of his future printed in his high school yearbook. Parseghian, a former assistant coach for Woody Hayes at Miami of Ohio who ascended to the head coaching position at Northwestern, was hired to return Notre Dame football to America's pedestal. It didn't take long. Parseghian willed the Irish back to their rightful place in college football with the same determination he displayed when he pursued the job after Hugh Devore left in 1964. By the end of that very first season when Notre Dame went 9–1 and Parseghian was named national coach of the year, Ara was not just known as the first non-Catholic, non-Notre Dame graduate to become head coach of the Irish. He was known as the answer to many a prayer.

Just two years into the glorious dawn of a new era in South Bend, Notre Dame won its first national title since the Leahy Era. Clearly, Notre Dame was again a national power. One game in that season—the famous 10–10 tie against Michigan State—best illustrated Parseghian's cunning and guile that made him unmatched in his profession. Parseghian understood that a loss that late in November would doom his title hopes, but a tie would keep them alive. So when the Irish regained the ball on their own thirty with just 1:24 left in the terrifically rugged game in East Lansing's wind-swept stadium, Parseghian opted to run out the clock rather than to risk losing the ball, the game, and the presumed national title.

Many Notre Dame fans didn't understand Parseghian's reasoning at the time, and many still don't. But with bad weather and a sophomore quarterback, Terry Hanratty, at the helm, Parseghian wouldn't risk a mistake; not with the Irish faithful so anxious for the national title.

"There's pressure in every coaching job, but winning makes it a lot easier to accept and fortunately we have been winning," Parseghian said that season. "But like one fan told me, 'we're with you, Ara, win or tie.' You notice he didn't say anything about losing." The truth is, losing wasn't part of many discussions during Parseghian's reign. In eleven years, his teams went 95–17–4, using a hands-on style that often found him on a blocking sled or a tackling dummy demonstrating technique to his rapt audience of

(top to bottom) Parseghian is carried off the field after beating Alabama in the 1973 Sugar Bowl. ■ Parseghian studies the action on the field.

(top to bottom) Parseghian accepts his Coach of the Year award from the NCAA in 1964. ■ A disgusted Devine argues with a referee.

players. Parseghian was a perfectionist, demanding even more of himself than the assistants who worked eighteen-hour days.

In 1973, that quest for perfection paid off in his only perfect season. It culminated in maybe one of the best college football games of the decade: a 24 to 23 victory over Paul "Bear" Bryant and Alabama in the Sugar Bowl. "This was not only a great game for Notre Dame, it was a great game for college football," Parseghian said. College football is always healthier when the Golden Dome shines brightly, and nobody in the game had quite the polish that Parseghian had. But rebuilding a dynasty takes its toll and only a year after his proudest moment at Notre Dame came his saddest.

Parseghian resigned at the end of the 1974 season, he said to preserve his physical and emotional health. The eleven seasons in South Bend had aged him in dog years, and he saw no choice but to bow out after winning ninety-five games and two national titles. To this day, Parseghian remains most often compared to Rockne for the tireless way he drove himself and his players and for the way he could stir the embers in a locker room that had lost its fire. Also like Rockne, he had set a nearly impossible standard of winning for his successors.

Dan Devine struggled to meet that standard, struggled to stack up to expectations that scraped the chin of Touchdown Jesus, at least in the discerning eyes of Notre Dame fans. Devine made his mark at Arizona State

and then Missouri before taking over the Green Bay Packers for four seasons. When Father Edmund Joyce called Devine, once Parseghian's fate was determined, Devine's surprise was only topped by the shock of Irish fans everywhere. To many Domers, Devine was an outsider and in many ways the anti-Ara. He seemed aloof and detached, even unimpressed by the aura of Notre Dame football that surrounded him. His football lineage could not be traced to Leahy or Rockne, and even though Parseghian's couldn't either, three national titles in eleven years had made everybody forget that. Devine didn't need to wake up the echoes; they were rustling in all their splendor. All he had to do was keep them stirring, and that meant winning. Immediately.

An 8–3 record in his first season followed by a 9–3 mark in his second wasn't good enough. It was 1977 and the thunder had begun to shake inside Devine's office. Ara, people were quick to note, hadn't lost his sixth game until his fifth season. The quality of Notre Dame football had begun to drop, fans fretted. Not that Devine let the lambasting affect him. "Pressure comes from within the family," he said before the '77 season. "There's no pressure hanging over our heads. We've got this guarded optimism." They also had this guy named Joe Montana.

If you wonder what puts Devine in the same company as Rockne, Leahy, and Parseghian, nothing explains it better than the decision Devine made September 24, 1977. He had nothing to base it on but his gut, which he trusted a lot more than Notre Dame fans did. So trailing Purdue 24 to 14 in the fourth quarter at Ross-Ade Stadium, Devine inserted quarterback Joe Montana, who had missed the entire 1976 season due to a shoulder separation. "Just a feeling," Devine would say.

After Montana rallied the Irish to a 31 to 24 victory, Devine was feeling even better. Montana gained a new nickname ("Comeback Joe"), Notre Dame

*Devine in the locker room
addressing the team*

legend gained another exciting chapter, and the national championship race gained another entry.

Devine stuck with Montana for the rest of the season and the Irish won eight straight, including another sterling fourth quarter comeback against Clemson in Death Valley.

Along the way, Devine also inspired another Notre Dame legend. After warming up in their usual blue jerseys against fifth-ranked USC, the Irish returned to the field in green jerseys prior to kickoff. The inspired Irish then trounced the Trojans 49 to 19. That set the Irish on their path to the Cotton Bowl opposite No. 1–ranked Texas, the country's only unbeaten team. At this point of the season, Devine had won back many of his detractors by turning the Irish into unlikely underdogs who defied the odds.

The underdog Irish romped over Texas 38 to 10 in the 1978 Cotton Bowl, a decisive win that cata-

pulted the Irish from fifth to first in the final polls. It was a season that began under the national microscope for Devine and ended in another Notre Dame national championship.

"We earned it on the field," Devine said. "We played No. 1 and beat them." It would be the pinnacle of a Notre Dame tenure that was marked by consistency, if not brilliance. His 53–16–1 record in six seasons made him proud, and Devine just might have stuck around long enough to chase another national title, but like Leahy and Parseghian, felt he had no choice but to leave. The health of his wife, Jo, had begun to fail, and Devine felt his place was with her. He left South Bend with a heavy heart and an unquestioned spirit.

Unlike Devine, Lou Holtz did not arrive in South Bend burdened by comparisons. The relative mediocrity of the Gerry Faust years only magnified every molecule of progress under Holtz. Fans saw the tempo and discipline with which the Irish played in

Holtz's first game and gained immediate hope—and that was a 24 to 23 loss to Michigan.

"I'm not the owner of a company here, I'm just the caretaker," Holtz said. "At most places the football coach feels like a czar. It's his team. Not at Notre Dame. I'm just here to keep an eye on things for a while." That was typical Holtz: self-deprecating without being defeatist; humble while still sounding strong, and woe to the Irish players who questioned that strength. Holtz immediately addressed the mental and physical fitness of the Irish, calling 6 A.M. winter workouts that reminded everyone how high the standard of the Notre Dame football player is.

(top to bottom) Holtz prepares his team.
■ *Holtz takes out his frustration.*

How high, you wonder? Holtz expected his Notre Dame men to behave like Notre Dame men twenty-four hours a day, seven days a week, no matter the circumstance. And if they didn't, they paid the consequences. Just ask Tony Brooks and Ricky Watters. The two were sophomore running backs and leading rushers on the 1988 Notre Dame team that eventually won the national championship. On the final game of that season, Holtz and the No. 1 Irish ventured to USC to face the rival No. 2–ranked Trojans. The showdown could not have been bigger, but it also represented the completion of the Notre Dame football renaissance that Holtz had begun. The Irish would need every last ounce of effort, and every last body.

Knowing this, Holtz still sent Watters and Brooks home from Los Angeles one day before the game because the two were late for a team meeting. The two had failed to meet the strict standard Holtz had established for his players, so they would watch the game on TV from South Bend. Their teammates would go to battle without them.

The Fighting Irish played fighting mad. Watters and Brooks weren't missed, and Holtz's point was made: no one is bigger than the Notre Dame program, a point driven home by a 27 to 10 Irish victory.

Tales like those define Holtz's legacy even more than his 100–30–2 record in eleven seasons, even more than the 1988 national championship that restored Notre Dame to prominence in college football's hierarchy. As masterful a football coach as Holtz was, he was becoming something of an icon among college coaches and ultimately bigger than the program he led. His was a complicated tenure, as compelling as it was successful.

It says everything about Lou Holtz that the people closest to him—coaches, friends, even some family members—remained unsure of his future plans just before his resignation on November 17, 1996. "I don't think anybody knows who I am," Holtz once said. "I don't know if I do." Holtz bathed in

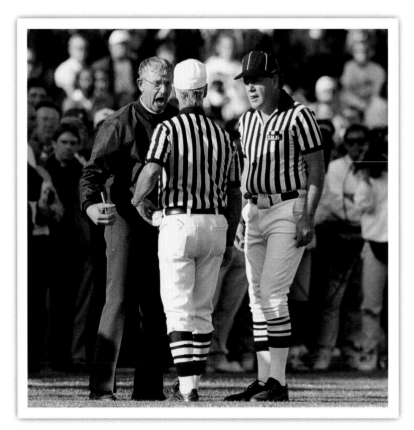

isolation. Standing at the podium, he could hold a ballroom full of executives in the palm of his hand. But sitting in a cozy room, he could feel uncomfortable casually talking to people with whom he is on a first-name basis. He found his comfort zone whenever he was leading a team meeting or watching game video by himself.

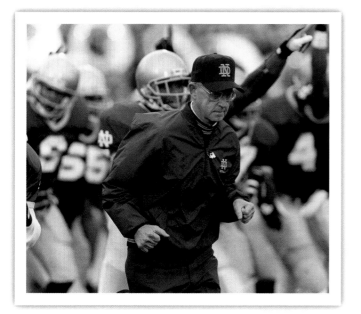

The circle around Holtz was tight, so observers learned not to take it personally when he breezed by with nary a wave or a nod. He liked to control every situation, and it was only when he lost the grip on the runaway train of rumors and innuendo that he decided to resign with a game left on the 1996 schedule instead of in mid-January, when he originally preferred. He kept the news media more than at arm's length, where many of his assistants also languished. More than a few former Notre Dame players have told stories of surviving four years of the Holtz regime without having one normal, relaxed conversation with their coach. But his training produced results.

"Notre Dame has more players in the NFL than any other college. I believe that is not by accident, nor do I believe it is predominantly because of talent.

The combination of hard work, discipline, fundamentals, intelligence, and character must be the cornerstone of any organization," Holtz said.

Being detached always worked for Holtz, but it struck a stark contrast with the man who could light up a TV studio with his magical one-liners or send busloads of Irish diehards home happy with a simple signature. He became a local legend and national attraction largely because of the command he held over the language, blending self-deprecating humor with God-fearing advice. His humility, at times, could seem like an act, but he was never dull.

The three national titles he promised were never realized, though in his heart he always will believe the Irish won championships in 1989 and 1993.

Holtz left Notre Dame with more intangible legacies, like restoring January to the Notre Dame football schedule and repairing the program to such an extent that NBC came calling with a national network television contract.

When he resigned, Holtz got up to the podium, his face lined like a road-map with stress, and said vaguely and simply, "It's the right thing to do." Nobody would know what he meant until a few months later when it was discovered that his wife, Beth, was suffering from cancer. Holtz needed his time to care for his ailing wife. In time, she would recover.

Without Lou, as with the departure of its other legendary coaches, Notre Dame would never be quite the same. Yet because of the proud traditions they have forged, Notre Dame's coaches have guaranteed that Notre Dame's place in collegiate football will remain unchanged and unequalled.

(left to right) A characteristically stoic Holtz leads his team out to face Ohio State. ■ Tim Grunhard lifts Coach Holtz in practice.

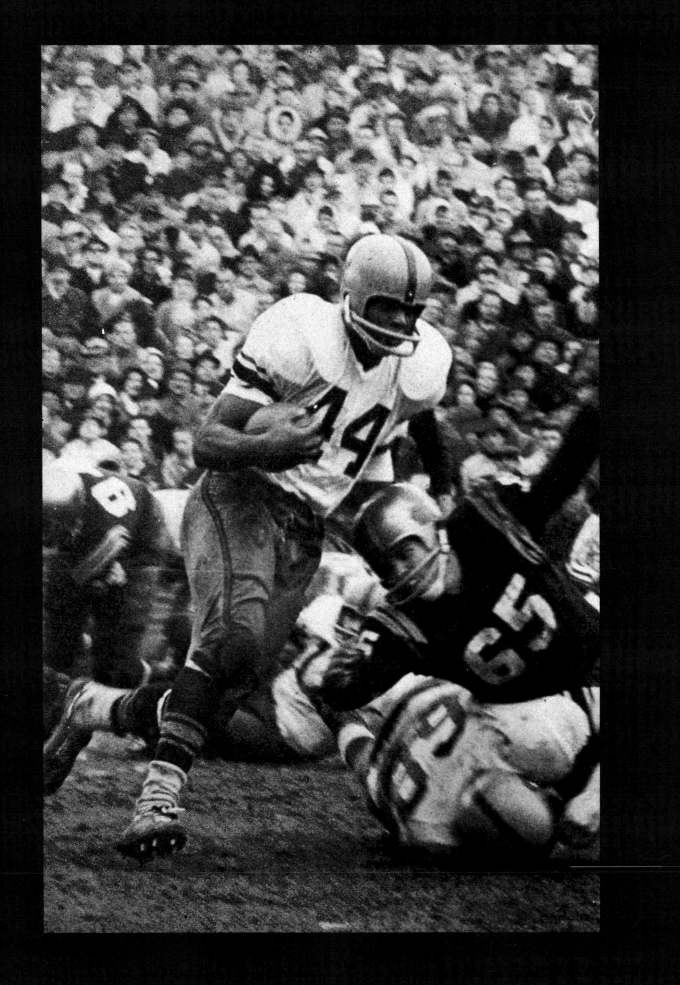

Perkowski Kicks Twice to Beat Syracuse

Notre Dame defeated Syracuse University, 17 to 15, on November 18, 1961, before a less-than-capacity crowd in South Bend. By this barren description, it was merely one victory in an unspectacular 5–5 Fighting Irish season.

The Orangemen entered the game ranked tenth in the country and had rallied late to take the lead 15 to 14. Notre Dame gained its final possession on its own thirty-yard line with just seventeen seconds left and no time-outs.

But a scramble by quarterback Frank Budka and a pass to George Sefcik moved the Irish to the Syracuse thirty-nine. Just three seconds remained. Coach Joe Kuharich called on straight-on kicker "Joe the Toe" Perkowski to attempt a preposterous fifty-six–yard field goal.

Jim Gibbons was at the mic for the Notre Dame radio network, "There's the pass from center …There's the kick! And it is no good!" Indeed, the kick was doomed, squibbed harmlessly by Perkowski. The game was over. Apparently.

But there was a flag on the field. Officials signaled a roughing-the-kicker penalty. The rules at the time read that as soon as a kicker boots the ball, there is a change of possession. By this strict definition, the flag was on the offensive team, since Perkowski had kicked the ball before being knocked to the turf.

A game can end on an offensive penalty, and since the clock now read 0:00, Syracuse thought it was secure in its victory.

But the officials determined that Notre Dame should get one more play. Fifteen yards were marked off and Perkowski had a second try—this time from forty-one yards. "There's the kick!…It's high enough…Is it through?…It's *good!*" exclaimed Gibbons. This kick was long and straight. Notre Dame had won 17 to 15.

Upon returning to New York, Syracuse athletic director Lew Andreas claimed victory. The Big Ten Conference and the East Coast Athletic Conference, who had jointly provided the officials, declared that the second kick came about erroneously because of a "misinterpretation of the rules." Newspapers throughout the East clamored for Notre Dame to surrender the victory.

Notre Dame president Fr. Theodore Hesburgh vowed to follow the determination of the NCAA rules committee and asked them to review the matter. But the committee wouldn't touch the issue and Syracuse gave up its fight.

The two teams have played only once since then. Notre Dame is scheduled to play at Syracuse's Carrier Dome on November 22, 2003—almost forty-two years to the day since Perkowski's double kick.

(left to right) Heisman winner Ernie Davis turns the corner on the Notre Dame defense. ■ *November 18, 1961, game program and ticket*

10–10 Tie for the National Championship

For over a month prior to the game, Notre Dame fans could smell an Irish classic in the making. No. 1–ranked Notre Dame, with a record of 8–0, was pitted against No. 2 Michigan State, with a record of 9–0, in a winner-take-all clash for the national championship.

The showdown took place on November 19, 1966, and thirty-three million viewers watched on ABC Television. The chilly reception from the 80,011 predominantly Spartan faithful made the freezing temperatures in East Lansing, Michigan, even colder for the visiting Irish. To add to their challenge, the crippled Notre Dame offense was up against one of the best Michigan State defensive teams in memory. While a brutal battle was expected, it was the strategy of the Irish in the final moments of the game that remains fiercely debated to this day. And despite the outcome, no one has

paid a greater price than Irish coach Ara Parseghian.

It was the host Spartans' final game of the season and they jumped out to a 10 to 0 second quarter lead. Before halftime, Irish running back Bob Gladieux scored Notre Dame's only touchdown of the game on a thirty-four–yard pass from Coley O'Brien. Notre Dame kicker Joe Azzaro's twenty-eight–yard field goal on the first play of the final quarter knotted the score at ten. Late in the game (there was no overtime in college football in 1966), Michigan State punted the ball back to Notre Dame one final time.

As Parseghian looked out over the field, he saw 1:24 remaining on the game clock, the score still knotted at ten apiece, and the football resting on the Notre Dame thirty-yard line.

The Michigan State defense stood across the line licking its chops. The Spartan defenders were a proud group, and they had every right to be. For two years running, they had been the nation's best. Now, for many of them, their collegiate careers had come down to eighty-four seconds. Due to existing Big Ten rules, a team was prohibited from appearing in the Rose Bowl two years in a row, so there would be no bowl game for undefeated Michigan State. It was now or never for Spartans Bubba Smith, George Webster, and their teammates.

(left to right) Tom O'Leary (40) is brought down by the Michigan State defense. ■ Quarterback Terry Hanratty (5) carries the ball for the Irish. ■ November 19, 1966, game program and ticket

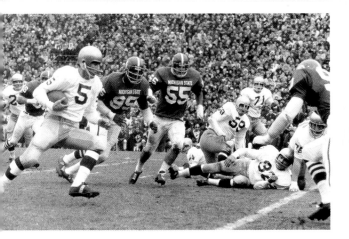

(left to right) Notre Dame's Jim Lynch brings down Dwight Lee after a one-yard gain in the first quarter. ■ Regis Cavender falls into the end zone for the only Michigan State touchdown. ■ MSU's Jess Phillips makes a desperate lunge as Bob Gladieux of Notre Dame scores the only Irish touchdown in the second quarter.

Notre Dame's backup quarterback, sophomore Coley O'Brien, had performed heroically after starter Terry Hanratty was knocked from the game with a shoulder injury by Bubba Smith in the second quarter. But O'Brien, a diabetic, was tiring. He'd missed seven straight pass attempts and was struggling to summon one last surge of energy.

Notre Dame's offense was in trouble. Not only was the apprentice O'Brien struggling mightily, the Irish had also lost All-American center George Goeddeke to injury earlier in the game; All-American halfback Nick Eddy missed the entire game with a shoulder injury; Eddy's replacement, Bob Gladieux, scored the game's only touchdown, but was later knocked out of the contest with a leg injury; another Notre Dame halfback, Rocky Bleier, sustained a lacerated kidney from a thunderous hit from behind by George Webster.

Besides all that, a strong northerly wind was howling at the back of the Michigan State defense, making a Notre Dame passing attack a risky proposition. In addition, if Michigan State got the ball back, the wind would aid one of the best field goal kickers in the country, Dick Kenney, ready and waiting on the Spartan sideline.

It had been an intense game for better than fifty-eight and one-half minutes. The Spartans were gen-

uinely outraged that any team, even the No. 1 team in the nation, could come back from a 10 to 0 deficit against them.

All game long, the teams had gone after each other relentlessly. The hitting, while nothing short of vicious, was clean. Not a single personal foul was called on either team. And in a game filled with spectacular plays, particularly on defense, the approach was businesslike on both sides. No signs of exuberance, no self-congratulatory plays to the national television cameras. It was two extraordinarily talented and proud football teams in the battle of their lives, prompting ABC's Chris Shenkel to comment, "Two teams that have all the array of weapons necessary for exciting offensive football and all the defensive giants necessary to stop attacks, here in the second half have reverted to kickin' the football."

And Parseghian, in his mind's eye, saw a larger battle. He saw that if he lost this battle, he had no chance to win the war. Notre Dame had set its sights nearly a year before on a national championship. He knew that giving up a score to the Spartans in the final seconds of the game would mean an end to that dream. While the Spartans were playing in their final game, the Irish had a date one week later at Southern California, ranked No. 10 in the nation. If the Irish, the reigning

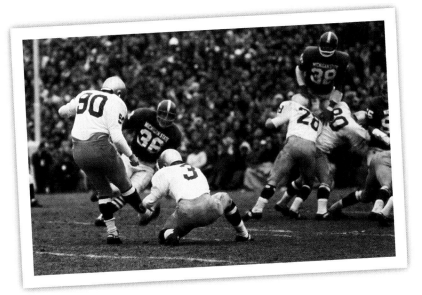

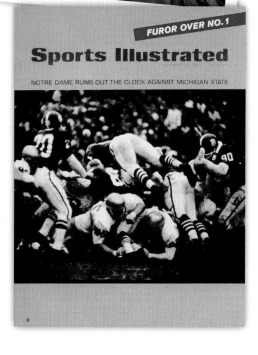

champs according to the polls, could stave off the Spartan challengers, they'd get another chance to make their case.

Parseghian tested every decision against one question: which option will give Notre Dame the best chance to win the national championship? It was that objective, and nothing else, that guided Parseghian's thinking. "There was only one way we could lose our chance to win the national championship, and that was by losing that game," says Parseghian. "Michigan State's season would be over and we still had one game left to play."

Parseghian ordered four straight running plays, including a quarterback sneak on fourth-and-one from his own thirty-nine–yard line, hardly a call for the faint of heart. After O'Brien's sneak got the ball to the Irish forty-one and gave Notre Dame a little breathing room, Parseghian called a pass. But All-American Bubba Smith sacked O'Brien for a seven-yard loss, pointedly underscoring Parseghian's contention that passing successfully on this drive was much easier said than done. O'Brien then kept the ball, running into the line on the game's final play. The game ended tied at 10.

Unfortunately for Parseghian, many writers and fans understandably didn't share his objective. Perhaps some were motivated by a desire for a winner and a loser in the much-anticipated game; perhaps others were influenced by an anti-Notre

Dame sentiment. In any event, Parseghian was mercilessly criticized.

"Some writer asked me why I didn't just have the quarterback throw the ball downfield out of bounds to make it look like we were trying to complete a long pass. Talk about hollowness, talk about phoniness," Parseghian snorted incredulously. "That was one of the most beautiful football games that has ever been played. What the writers and the general public wanted was a winner out of this ballgame. The strategy that we employed is one that I have absolutely no regret about."

The logic and wisdom of Parseghian's decision was validated in the season's final polls. While the coaches poll moved the Spartans ahead of Notre Dame after the tie (the media poll left Notre Dame No. 1), both polls voted Notre Dame No. 1 in their final rankings following Notre Dame's season-ending 51 to 0 trouncing of Southern California the following week. Parseghian and his team had reached their objective, and nothing else mattered, especially the squawking of a bevy of armchair quarterbacks.

As the Notre Dame and Michigan State players trudged off the field that day, despite the incredible frustration of a 10 to 10 tie, there were many heroes among them. But no hero stood taller and more confident in his decision than Ara Parseghian.

(left to right) Notre Dame kicker Joe Azzaro ties the game at 10. ■ The end of the game found Notre Dame and Michigan State tied. ■ Notre Dame coach Ara Parseghian (left) walks off the field with Michigan State coach Duffy Daugherty after their teams battled to a 10 to 10 tie at Spartan Stadium. ■ A Sports Illustrated *cover featuring the "Furor over No. 1."*

Theismann
Runs Over No. 1 Texas

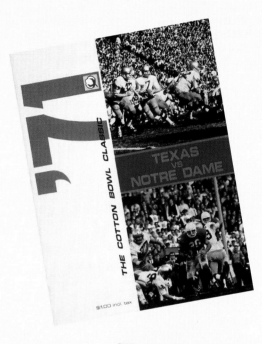

After waiting forty-five years—from 1925 to 1970—between its first and second bowl games, Notre Dame's football team didn't have to wait nearly as long for a third bowl appearance. The Irish, who had nearly upset top-ranked Texas in the 1970 Cotton Bowl, earned a rematch in the same venue in 1971. Once again, the Longhorns were undefeated and sitting atop the polls.

Notre Dame's 1970 squad had title aspirations of its own, but they were dealt a severe blow in the final game of the regular season in Los Angeles. Southern California had spoiled Notre Dame's perfect season with a 38 to 28 upset, despite Irish quarterback Joe Theismann's heroics—a performance featuring 526 passing yards that still stands as a school record. The Irish national championship hopes were all but washed away in a driving rainstorm.

As Notre Dame and Texas practiced in preparation for round two, the buzz was impossible to miss. Nobody ever accused Texas fans of being bashful, and now they had a lot to boast about—their Longhorns were riding a thirty-game winning streak. In the minds of the Texas faithful, the '71 Cotton Bowl was to be a coronation. It was as if Notre Dame was there simply to play the role of the Washington Generals to Texas's Harlem Globetrotters act. Theismann recalls thinking that Notre Dame still had a chance to win the national championship. But the sixth-ranked Irish would need to beat Texas and be the beneficiaries of a number of extremely unlikely scenarios in order to vault to the top of the polls. The reality was, Notre Dame was playing for little more than pride.

It was more than enough.

Irish coach Ara Parseghian and his staff were convinced that the effort of Notre Dame's defense, while valiant in the '70 battle, would have to be much more effective to turn the tables. After all, the Longhorns had run for a whopping 331 yards and picked up nineteen rushing first downs the previous year.

(left to right) Joe Theismann breaks away from a Longhorn tackler on his way to the end zone in the first quarter. ■ Senior quarterback Joe Theismann poses for an action photo. ■ 1971 Cotton Bowl program and ticket stub

(left to right) Theismann turns the corner with the blocking help of Ed Gulyas. ■ Theismann hands off to halfback Larry Parker.

"We knew that we wouldn't be able to use our standard defense against them," Parseghian explained. "We came up with a mirror defense, which in effect made them play left-handed."

In essence, the Irish deployed their players to mirror the Longhorn formations, throwing their blocking assignments and timing into disarray.

To say the scheme worked would be a monumental understatement. Notre Dame's defense forced Texas to fumble nine times—not counting the national championship hardware the Longhorns left lying on the ground.

Although Texas quarterback Eddie Phillips scampered for 164 yards, he did so because Notre Dame shut down every other option. Running back Steve Worster, who punished the Irish for 155 yards on twenty carries the previous year, managed just forty-two yards on sixteen carries. Jim Bertelsen, who gained eighty-one yards on eighteen carries in the '70 contest, was held to eight yards on five carries.

And while the Irish defense was suffocating the Longhorns' attack, Theismann broke their backs. In a 9:30 span over the first and second quarter, the

Irish quarterback ran for two touchdowns and threw for another.

First in that string of scores, Theismann looked to cap a ten-play, eighty-yard drive. "Alright, it's fourth down and two to go for Notre Dame. Theismann has been to the bench to talk with Parseghian. They're not going to try for a field goal, they're going to go for a first down," said Connie Alexander, calling the game on CBS Radio. "Here they are in a 'power-I,' both ends tight…Theismann back to pass from the thirty-five…Fires!…Complete at the ten to Gatewood who makes the grab!…And Gatewood is at the five and into the end zone!…He gets a touchdown for Notre Dame!" Split end Tom Gatewood, Theismann's favorite receiver, was No. 2 in the nation that year in pass receptions, and had come through again. After an extra point kick, Notre Dame led 7 to 3, and the Longhorns never recovered.

Texas fumbled the ensuing kickoff, giving Notre Dame the ball on the Longhorns thirteen. Theismann's one-yard keeper on fourth-and-one at the Texas four kept the drive alive. Two plays later, he took it in from the three for a 14 to 3 Irish lead with over five minutes still to play in the first quarter.

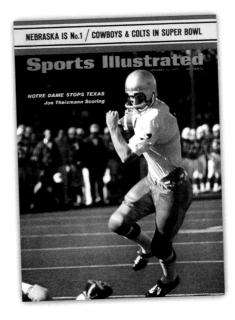

Notre Dame players were more than aware that Texas had roared back from a 10 to 0 first quarter deficit a year earlier. This game was far from over.

Barely six minutes later, Theismann took care of that.

The Irish defense forced Texas to punt from the Longhorns thirteen after a three-and-out series, and Notre Dame took over on its own forty-seven. After a nineteen-yard pass to tight end Mike Creaney, the Irish kept it on the ground. On second-and-seven from the Texas fifteen, Theismann combined sleight-of-hand, quick feet, balance, and a little power. After faking a handoff and eluding one tackler in the backfield, Theismann headed around the right end, just as he had done on his first touchdown and his fourth-down run that set up the earlier scoring run.

Again, Alexander called it, "Here we go on second down and seven to go…and it's a keeper by Theismann!…He's down to the ten…" Theismann didn't encounter another defender until linebacker Stan Mauldin closed in near the Texas five. "Down to the five…tightroping along the far sideline!" Somehow, the 6 foot, 170 pounder stayed on his feet and inbounds. "Touchdown for Theismann who miraculously stayed in bounds along the far sideline!" An extra point kick from Scott Hempel put Notre Dame ahead 21 to 3, and they wouldn't relinquish that lead.

"Our defense and our offensive line were the most dominant factors in the game," says Theismann, who had set Cotton Bowl records for passing and total yards in the 1970 heartbreaker. This time, though, he walked off the field with the victory while his losing counterpart Phillips broke Theismann's year-old records for passing yardage and total offense.

"The pride factor came from the fact that we had lost to them the year before," Theismann says. "Whether the game was for the national championship or not didn't matter.

"I was so sick of hearing 'Hook 'em Horns,'" says Theismann, referring to the battle cry of the Texas faithful.

Theismann and the Irish administered a good, old-fashioned whipping to the Longhorns, ruining their party and stopping their winning streak at thirty with a 24 to 11 upset. Later that night, Nebraska clinched the national championship by defeating LSU 17 to 12 in the Orange Bowl. The Irish finished No. 2.

For Theismann, his final collegiate game was both a culmination of his Irish years and a preview of the Super Bowl–winning NFL career ahead of him. For the Irish, it was about ignoring the odds and the skeptics; it was about perseverance; it was about winning. Most of all, it was about pride.

(left to right) Joe Theismann rushes for one of his two touchdowns in the Irish upset. ■ *All-American quarterback Joe Theismann's domination of the Longhorns was featured on the cover of* Sports Illustrated. ■ *A victorious Parseghian is carried off the field by Irish players.*

The Trojan War:
The Notre Dame–
USC Rivalry

When Notre Dame rallied to beat the University of Southern California by the score of 13 to 12 in 1926, Irish coach Knute Rockne called it "the greatest game I ever saw." All USC Trojans coach Howard Jones could say to Rockne in the middle of the Los Angeles Coliseum field was a curt, obligatory, "Congratulations." Congratulations, of course, were in order for both of these coaching legends for starting what quickly became the greatest intersectional rivalry in college football.

Beginning with that 1926 game, when little-used Irish quarterback Art Parisien flipped the winning pass to halfback Johnny Niemiec, the two teams have met on the gridiron seventy-two times—many of them pigskin classics. Over the years, no other series has featured more national championships on the line, more Heisman Trophy winners on the field, or more football fans in front of their television sets. Nine times since the first poll was started in 1936, one of the two teams was ranked No. 1 during their clash. Fourteen times during the series, one of the two teams went on to win the national championship. And in both 1938 and 1964, the Trojans thwarted top-ranked Irish teams from finishing undefeated.

Between the two teams, there have been eras of domination and teams of dynasty, but never a hint of dullness in this annual series that has occurred nearly continuously since 1926, stopping for just

three years during World War II. The names of the heroes and coaches have changed over the years. Even the Notre Dame jersey colors suddenly changed to green before kickoff one afternoon in 1977. But green jerseys or not, the intensity and the pride that go with this rivalry have remained constant.

Appreciating the rich history of the series firsthand, Lou Holtz once said, "'Southern Cal.' That's all you have to say." That's pretty much all Knute Rockne had to say some sixty years earlier. Not only had Rockne arranged the matchup of cross-country powers, Rockne was instrumental in getting USC to hire Howard Jones as coach. As Irish luck would have it, Rockne himself had declined the USC job offer.

On their second trip west to play USC in 1928, Rockne invited members of the press to watch his team practice in Tucson, Arizona. He was miffed to find key elements of his game plan exposed in the Los Angeles papers. "It serves me right to be nice to certain sportswriters," Rockne said, after his team lost 27 to 14 to the Trojans.

(left to right) Notre Dame's Michael Stonebreaker, Wes Prichett, and Todd Lyght stop Aaron Emanuel at the goal line in 1988. ■ Three USC players bring down Notre Dame halfback Bob Saggau after a two-yard gain in 1940.

(left to right) Notre Dame coach Terry Brennan on the sidelines during the 1955 game against USC. ■ USC Coach Howard Jones prepares his team for the game against Notre Dame in 1932. Pictured left to right are Bob Erskine, Gordon Clark, Homer Griffith, Howard Jones, and Robert McNeish.

Rockne showed his cunning two years later when he had swift halfback Bucky O'Connor pretend to be slow-footed during practice on the way out to play USC. O'Connor even intentionally fumbled the ball a few times. The press took the bait and so did USC. With the Trojans keying on the other players in the Irish backfield, O'Connor ran wild in a 27 to 0 Irish victory. The spirited shutout would be Rockne's last game. He died the following March in a plane crash, yet his legend and legacy live on—including the Notre Dame–USC series he started.

In 1948, a confident Irish team rallied late against the Trojans for a 14 to 14 tie to keep their longest unbeaten streak alive (which would eventually reach a then-record thirty-nine games). A Red Sitko touchdown run with just thirty-five seconds left on the clock, followed by a Steve Oracko extra point, did the trick. Notre Dame's Bill Gay set up the crucial score in that game when he returned a kickoff eighty-six yards to the USC thirteen-yard line. Before his scamper, Gay had turned to an official and asked how much time was left in the game. When he was told that 2:35 remained, he said, "Time enough, sir."

The Irish–Trojan rivalry reached its pinnacle in the '60s and '70s when Ara Parseghian coached the Irish and John McKay coached USC. During the "Era of Ara," from 1964 to 1974, the two teams won a combined five national championships, and almost won a sixth. But in Parseghian's first year as the Irish head coach in 1964, USC rallied from a 17 to 0 halftime deficit to hand the top-ranked and 9–0 Irish a heartbreaking 20 to 17 defeat. The winning touchdown was scored with just 1:33 to play on a fourth-down, fifteen-yard pass from Craig Fertig to Rod Sherman. Understandably, there was plenty of emotion when USC came to Notre Dame the following year. The Irish avenged the disappointment of the previous year, winning 28 to 7.

One year later, the Irish ensured their selection as 1966 national champion by bouncing back from a 10 to 10 tie with Michigan State to wallop the (left to right) Jim Morse of Notre Dame takes a Paul Hornung pass for a twenty-four–yard gain during the first quarter of the USC game in 1955. ■ USC half-back O.J. Simpson dives over the center of the Notre Dame line to score during the fourth quarter in 1967.

Trojans in the Coliseum, 51 to 0. It was USC's worst defeat ever. McKay praised the Notre Dame effort and then consoled his own team by telling them, "Forget it. There are seven hundred million Chinese who don't even know we played." Unfortunately for the Trojans, millions of football fans in this country did know.

When the teams played to a 21 to 21 tie two years later in 1968, it was the highest-rated regular season college game ever shown on television. Three other contests from the series still rank in the top six. McKay may have said "Forget it," after that devastating USC loss in 1966—but that certainly was easier said than done. Over the next sixteen seasons, the Trojans fashioned a 12–2–2 record against the Irish, including a 7–0–1 mark at the Coliseum. Ironically, the only two Notre Dame victories in that span (in 1973 and 1977) catapulted the Irish to national titles.

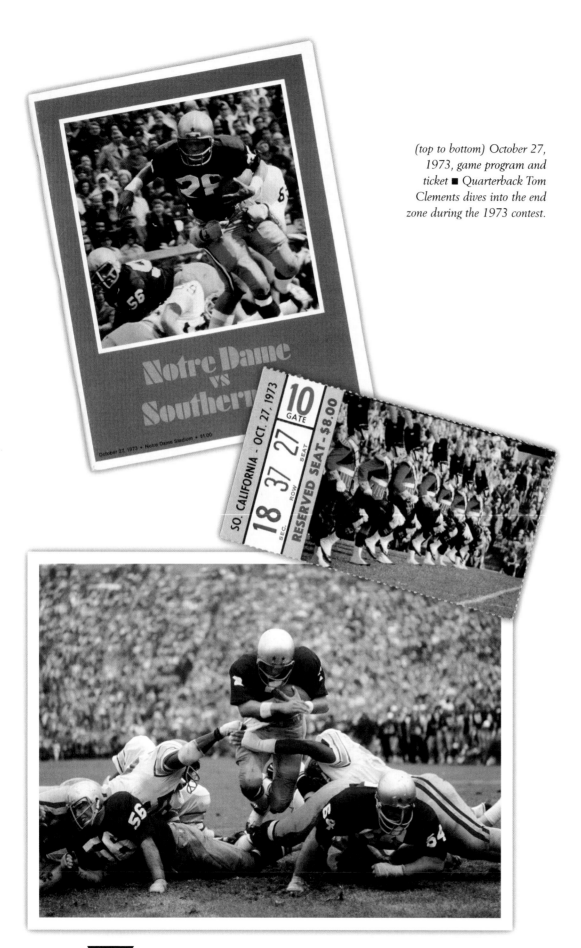

(top to bottom) October 27, 1973, game program and ticket ■ Quarterback Tom Clements dives into the end zone during the 1973 contest.

In 1972, USC sophomore tailback Anthony Davis scored six touchdowns, two on kickoff returns, and did a little end zone dance after each one in a heart-breaking 45 to 23 USC victory. Riled Notre Dame students taped Davis's picture to sidewalks around the Notre Dame campus before the 1973 matchup to allow students to stomp on him on the way to class. "His name still makes me flinch," Parseghian recently said of Davis.

Going into that 1973 game, both teams were unde-feated. They met on a rainy October afternoon in South Bend, and emotions were at a fever pitch. On the first play from scrimmage, USC flanker Lynn Swann awaited a little swing pass from quarterback Pat Haden while Irish freshman safety Luther Bradley bore down on him. The ball and Bradley got to Swann at the same time and it looked as if Bradley might have beheaded Swann. But it was only his empty helmet—and the gauntlet—that hit the ground with Swann. Irish cornerback Tim Rudnick had his own message for Anthony Davis after a tackle early in the game. "This isn't the Coliseum," Rudnick said as he looked down into Davis's face mask. "This is South Bend. So pick your tail up and get back in the huddle."

With the Irish leading 13 to 7, Parseghian hoped to break the game open at the start of the second half. With the ball deep in their own territory, Parseghian called for a ground attack. He pulled both of his guards to the left and had quarterback Tom Clements fake a handoff to fullback Wayne Bullock before pitching the ball to Eric Penick. Penick, a state champion sprinter from Cleveland, was hardly touched as he headed left and broke away from all-American linebacker Richard Wood before out-rac-ing two USC defensive backs to the end zone on his eighty-five–yard scamper.

"After my block I can still remember seeing No. 44 (Penick) going down the field like twin pistons," said Notre Dame guard and team captain Frank Pomarico. "It was like the ground was shaking below me." Parseghian, who was a spry fifty years of age at

(left to right) Halfback Eric Penick charges upfield after a handoff from Clements. ■ Coach Ara Parseghian with quarterback Tom Clements in 1973

the time, took off down the sidelines himself when it was obvious that it was going to be a big play. He almost beat Penick to the goal line as he cheered on his halfback. "I almost joined him in the end zone," Parseghian later said. The Irish went on to win that game 23 to 14, and were on their way to their ninth national title.

The tides turned in 1974, when the Trojans got their revenge by scoring fifty-five unanswered points in a seventeen-minute span after the Irish had taken a 24 to 0 lead late in the first half. Davis was sensational again, opening the floodgates by returning the second-half kickoff for a devastating touchdown. "Boy, I got tired of seeing that horse on days like that," said Parseghian of USC mascot Traveler, who was ridden up and down the sidelines after every USC score in the Coliseum. "We had some great games with USC and some wild ones, too," Parseghian reminisced. "You just never knew what to expect. How can you explain a 51 to 0 victory over them in the Coliseum (in 1966) and that total disaster on our part in the second half of 1974?"

(left to right) October 22, 1977, game program and ticket ■ Notre Dame, sporting green jerseys, scores against USC in 1977.

In 1977, Notre Dame coach Dan Devine managed his only victory over USC in six tries. In Rockne-esque fashion, he secretly ordered green jerseys for his team before the season and decided to unveil them just before the USC game. The Irish, ranked No. 1 at the start of the season, had been upset by Ole Miss in the second game and needed a lift to get back into national contention when USC came to town. Only the captains knew of the switch until the rest of the team returned to the locker room after pregame warm-ups.

Notre Dame fans were overcome by the site of their green-clad lads, and the millions of Domers watching on ABC Television listened to commentator Keith Jackson describe the exciting emotional scene, "You've heard the reference about a 'green machine,' look at the jerseys! That's the Notre Dame football team for the first time wearing green." The crowd was going wild. "You talk about stretching emotions. Looking for an asset. Finding any advantage. Whatever it takes....Listen to this crowd!" The green jerseys worked like a charm. "The reaction was unbelievable," said defensive

(left to right) USC Coach John Robinson on the sidelines during Notre Dame's 1977 rout ■ The "wearing of the green"

back Nick DeCicco. "It was better than any pep talk any coach ever gave in the history of the game." The Irish won the contest 49 to 19. "How did you like our early St. Patrick's Day celebration?" laughed defensive coordinator Joe Yonto after the victory. Devine gave his psychological ploy only so much credit. "Let's get underneath them," he said. "There's an awful lot of heart under those jerseys."

The Trojans proceeded to win the rivalry the next five years in a row, tying the longest winning streak in the series. The last time it had been accomplished was by the Irish during the Frank Leahy era in the 1940s. But the rivalry would quickly turn again in Notre Dame's favor. And in a big way. From 1983 until 1995, the Irish would go 12–0–1 against USC, including winning eleven years in a row. It was a stretch of domination that defied the wildest prognostication and went counter to the storied history of two proud programs. In five of those games, the Trojans had even been favored.

First year coach Lou Holtz brought his 1986 Fighting Irish team to the Los Angeles Coliseum with a dismal 4–6 record. USC quickly took command of the game, and with four minutes to play in the third quarter, the Irish found themselves down 30 to 12. But the Irish rallied with three touchdowns and an astonishing fifty-six–yard punt return by Tim Brown, a thrilling moment in Irish history that Tony Roberts and Tom Pagna, the voices of Notre Dame on Westwood One Radio, excitedly described for their audience of Irish faithful, "Here's the kick—high—Tim Brown settling under it. At the twenty-eight…circles to the right—breaks the tackle! Gets to the thirty! To the thirty-five! Down the sideline at the forty! Forty-five! All the way down the sideline, thirty! Twenty-five! Twenty! Fifteen-yard line!" The stadium erupted. "Everything green in this stadium is absolutely rockin'!" added Pagna. Brown's charge put Notre

Dame within range for John Carney's nineteen-yard field goal as the clock ran down to pull out the 38 to 37 victory. It was the first time the Irish had beaten USC in the last minute of a game.

That 1986 game was a fitting ending for Carney and quarterback Steve Beuerlein, who engineered Notre Dame's comeback and also held Carney's winning kick. Carney, who had set kicking records at Notre Dame, had nonetheless missed two earlier game-ending field goal attempts that would have beaten Michigan and Pitt. Beuerlein had become Notre Dame's career leading passer, but was almost yanked by Holtz in the USC game after an interception. The game turned his way, though, as he went on to tie a school record with four touchdown passes. Tim Brown's outstanding performance on the day (he had a forty-nine–yard pass reception and a fifty-seven–yard kickoff return along with his crucial fifty-six–yard punt return at game's end) officially started the campaign for his Heisman Trophy the next season. He would become the eleventh Heisman winner—seven from Notre Dame and four from USC—to play in this historic series. Maybe more important, the 1986 victory helped propel the struggling Irish back into national contention.

Just two years later, an undefeated Notre Dame team would beat an undefeated Southern California team en route to its 1988 national championship. Surprisingly, the matchup was the only time in the history of this great rivalry that the teams were ranked No. 1 and No. 2 when they played. Amidst a cloud of controversy after Lou Holtz suspended two of the team's leading rushers, Tony Brooks and Ricky Watters, for showing up late for a team meeting, the Irish rose to the occasion with a dominating victory.

(left to right) Stan Smagala intercepted a Rodney Peete pass late in the first half and returned it sixty-four yards for a touchdown in the 1988 game. ■ Tony Rice breaks loose on the option.

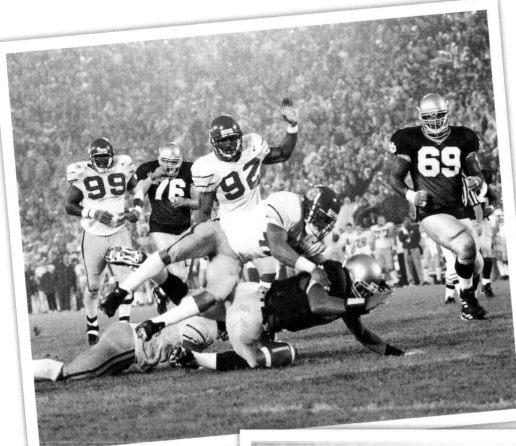

While big plays like the opening fifty-five–yard pass play from Notre Dame's own end zone by Tony Rice to Raghib Ismail and Rice's sixty-five–yard option run for a touchdown in the first quarter kept the Trojan defense on their toes, it was the Irish defense that delivered the victory. The defensive line put pressure on USC's celebrated quarterback Rodney Peete all day. Frank Stams took matters into his own hands, leading the Irish with nine tackles, two-and-a-half sacks, a fumble recovery, and a bone-crushing block on Peete after a key interception by Irish cornerback, Stan Smagala. With fifty-two seconds left in the first half, Smagala intercepted Peete's first-down pass and bolted down the sideline for a sixty-four–yard touchdown. In the midst of the play, Stams landed a monstrous hit on Peete. In one single play, both emotionally and physically, the Trojans were beat. The Irish went into halftime with a 20 to 7 lead and emerged at game's end with a 27 to 10 victory on the way to their eleventh national championship.

(top to bottom) Jarious Jackson fumbles in the end zone in 1999. ■ *Jabari Holloway recovered Jackson's fumble for an Irish score.*

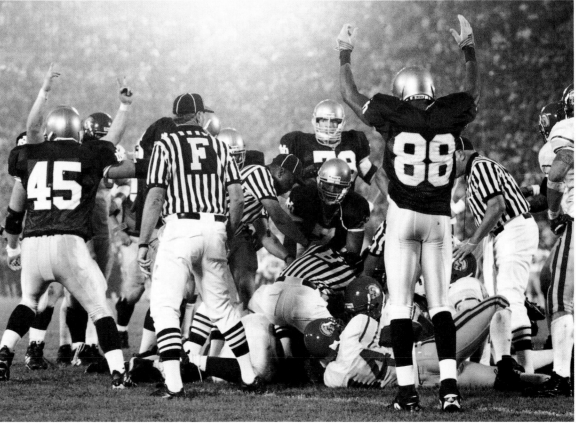

As recently as 1999, and true to form for this historic rivalry, the Fighting Irish rebounded from a 24 to 3 deficit midway through the third quarter in monsoon-like conditions to beat the Trojans 25 to 24. The twenty-one–point comeback was among the greatest in the history of Notre Dame Stadium. When the Irish changed directions at the start of the fourth quarter, the wind curiously seemed to do the same thing behind them. "Someone elbowed me and said, 'Now, they've changed the wind, too,'" said USC Coach Paul Hackett. "That's what happens when you play at Notre Dame Stadium."

The winning touchdown was scored with 2:40 left in the game when Irish quarterback Jarious Jackson fumbled the ball just before the goal line and, as Irish luck would have it, teammate Jabari Holloway fell on it in the end zone for the score.

The storylines change over the years, but the rivalry and tradition continue. Players and fans never lose the intense desire to win this one game above all others. Sixty years after Rockne and Jones shared a curt handshake when the series began, a hand was offered to Lou Holtz to shake after the 1986 Irish comeback victory against the Trojans. Holtz took it. "Welcome to the rivalry, Coach," said former USC player Anthony Davis, probably Notre Dame's all-time greatest nemesis.

Notre Dame and USC. Fierce competitors. Respected foes. Historic rivals.

Fighting Irish and Trojans battle in the trenches.

Clements and the Irish Beat 'Bama in the 1973 Sugar Bowl

Notre Dame quarterback Tom Clements, a cold-blooded kind of competitor, actually flinched a little when his coach, Ara Parseghian, gave him the play call. "I think it was the first time that I saw Tom Clements look surprised," said Irish backfield coach Tom Pagna. There was good reason. Nursing a 24 to 23 lead in the waning moments of the 1973 Sugar Bowl, the Irish faced a third-and-six situation from inside their own five-yard line. Parseghian called for a pass to tight end Dave Casper. Despite the wind in their faces, despite a No. 1 Alabama defense revved up to make a game-changing stop with 2:12 remaining, and despite Clements being just a misstep away from a safety and losing the lead, Parseghian called for a pass.

Pagna later admitted he was surprised, too. "I remember asking Ara if he really had called that play and he said, 'Hell yes, I did.' What could I say? I told Ara it was a good call." Clements, who had led the Irish to a 10–0 regular season, also wanted to check that his hearing was working properly. "I do remember asking Coach Parseghian if he was sure he wanted that play," he said. Parseghian wasn't holding back. Neither were his players. "The call didn't surprise me," said offensive guard Frank Pomarico, one of the captains that season.

Even so, Parseghian may have been concealing his own question about the call. "My biggest worry was that Tom might get tackled or slip in the end zone for a safety," he said. "He always has such confidence in his running ability." The entire Irish backfield had shown off their running ability early in the game, gaining 118 yards on the ground against Alabama in the first quarter alone.

But their most astonishing feat came in the second quarter. Alabama kicked off to the Irish and halfback Al Hunter. Chris Shenkel, Bud Wilkinson, and Howard Cosell called the game for ABC Television, and Shenkel excitedly counted off the yardage as Hunter pulled in the ball and broke loose on a dazzling return. "Al Hunter at the fifteen for Notre Dame. At the thirty! At the thirty-five! Forty! Midfield, look at him go! Ninety-four yards and a Notre Dame touchdown!" As Hunter crossed the goal line, the Irish poured from the sidelines into the

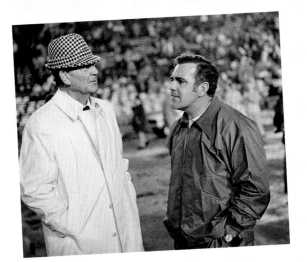

(left to right) Clements, throwing from the end zone, completes a pass to Robin Weber. ■ Alabama coach Paul "Bear" Bryant and Notre Dame coach Ara Parseghian exchange friendly words before the game. ■ Game program and ticket from the 1973 Sugar Bowl

A rocky start marked the fourth quarter, with three turnovers in ninety seconds. But Alabama got on track, as second-string quarterback Richard Todd handed off to halfback Mike Stock at the Irish twenty-five. Todd charged up the sidelines, positioning himself for a return pass from Stock, and then ran it in for a touchdown. Although the Tide missed the conversion attempt, Alabama held the lead for a third time, 23 to 21.

The lead swung again as kicker Bob Thomas put the Irish up with a nineteen-yard field goal with 5:13 remaining. The kick was good by only a couple of feet. "If I stuck it down the pipe, nobody would have remembered it," Thomas later said. Alabama's next possession failed, forcing them to punt. After Alabama punter Gary Gantt got off a marvelous sixty-nine–yard punt to the Notre Dame one with three minutes remaining, make-or-break time had arrived.

Two running plays netted less than four yards for the Irish. Parseghian knew that if the Irish didn't get a first down, the Crimson Tide would have great field position and plenty of time to get in position for a game-winning field goal. "I thought a pass would take them by surprise, especially if we were in a two–tight end situation," Parseghian later said. "We had the wind against us and we had noticed that the end zone sloped back and down. It would have been very difficult for our punter, Brian Doherty, to get it out of there."

Assistant coach Wally Moore had even gone so far as to use a string during a practice to discover that the back of the end zone was nine inches lower than the front. "That would have been like punting out of a hole," Moore said. The Irish dug themselves a little deeper into their own hole as the crucial play was about to unfold. Clements strung out a long count, hoping to draw Alabama offsides.

"Alabama did jump offsides," Parseghian said. "But so did Casper. I wanted offsides called on both teams so there would be nullifying penalties. But

end zone to celebrate with him. "Oh! Have we got a football game!" shouted Cosell. Notre Dame led 12 to 7, and Parseghian instructed his Irish squad to "Go for two." Clements' pass to split end Pete Demmerle barely made it over the fingertips of Alabama defender Wayne Rhodes. The Irish led 14 to 7.

Notre Dame couldn't help but be pleased with their lead and their ability to run on a slick field while wearing someone else's cleats. Rain had fallen in New Orleans for hours before the game. The Irish players had to leave their new blue-and-gold shoes in their lockers and wear ones with shorter cleats that equipment manager Gene O'Neill had borrowed from Tulane University at the last minute.

Alabama players, though, came back with their own fancy footwork. A thirty-nine–yard field goal from Bill Davis made a dent in the Irish lead. Then a ninety-three–yard march in eleven plays, capped by a five-yard scoring push by Wilbur Jackson, put Alabama back in the lead. But the pendulum swung again when Notre Dame linebacker Drew Mahalic ran back an Alabama fumble to the Tide's twelve-yard line. Eric Penick followed with a score, putting the Irish ahead 21 to 17.

(top to bottom) Quarterback Tom Clements calls the play from scrimmage. ■ Alabama's Bill Davis splits the uprights with a thirty-nine–yard field goal in the third quarter.

they marked it off against us." That put the ball back to the three-yard line. Clements looked over to the sidelines and was given the "Repeat" sign—same play.

Alabama may not have expected a pass, but its defense still had the All-American Casper well covered. So Clements turned his head to see Robin Weber, the second tight end, break open on the left sideline. Despite the fact that Weber hadn't caught a pass during the entire regular season, Clements went with his only option. "Third down. Clements coming up. It's a pass!" Shenkel said with excitement. Clements pumped, faked, pumped, and then threw from his own end zone hitting Weber for a thirty-five–yard gain. "He's got his man! Robin Weber, number 91, a sopho-more from Dallas, Texas!" Shenkel shouted. "Give Tommy Clements all the credit in the world!" Cosell added. "We said at the top of the show, he was a young man who was not afraid to throw. That his favorite receiver was Demmerle, he proved that out. That his second favorite receiver was Casper, he proved that out. And now to number 91, what a clutch play!"

It was over. The Irish had the first down and then ran out the clock for the one-point victory and the national championship.

"That pass really caught us by surprise," said Mal Moore, an Alabama assistant who would later serve as assistant head coach at Notre Dame. "It was a

very good call—a gutsy call. I think Coach Bryant and the rest of us thought we had Notre Dame in a posi-tion in which we could have won the game. And I think Ara sensed that."

"I just think the fact that we were in a two–tight end situation gave Alabama the idea we were going to run," Parseghian said.

After the game, Bryant hunted down Clements in the victorious Notre Dame locker room. "It was very crowded but he came over and con-gratulated me," Clements said. "I thought that was very nice of him."

Bryant was gracious in defeat but obviously disap-pointed. "I thought we'd win it all the way, especially with the wind in the fourth quarter," he said. "If I'd been a betting man, I would have bet on that."

"I think Notre Dame is a great team," the Alabama coaching legend continued, "but I wouldn't mind playing them tomorrow. In fact, I'd like that."

The Irish only were interested in savoring their vic-tory. "I was sitting in the locker room and my dad and grandfather and brother were sitting there beside me," captain Pomarico recalled. "It was a cold and rainy night outside. But in all my life I've never felt warmer."

(left to right) Clements hands off to fullback Wayne Bullock (30). ■ Halfback Al Hunter finds a hole in the Alabama defense. ■ The struggling Alabama defense stops a Notre Dame run.

End of an "Ara": The 1975 Orange Bowl

During one lopsided Notre Dame victory in South Bend, a drenched student body started chanting, "Ara, stop the rain! Ara, stop the rain!" The legendary Irish coach heard them. He turned to his assistant coach, Tom Pagna, and kiddingly asked, "Do you think I should?" They laughed, and the rain eventually ended. On January 1, 1975, at Miami's Orange Bowl, Ara Parseghian's sensational reign at Notre Dame was about to end as well.

The "Era of Ara," they called it—a marvelous eleven-year run that had produced two national championships, nine top ten finishes, and what would be a 95–17–4 overall record. So it seemed a strange scenario that his last hurrah as the Notre Dame coach would find his Irish as eleven-point underdogs to No. 1 Alabama and trying to rebound from a devastating 55 to 24 loss to rival USC in the last regular season game. "Even some eternal optimists weren't giving us a very good chance in that game," Parseghian later said.

The season had taken its toll. Parseghian, looking drained and drawn, was only fifty-one when he decided to walk away from coaching after the 1974 season, his twenty-fourth straight as a head coach. He was just worn out. After winning the 1973 national title and with seventeen starters returning, expectations for the '74 season had been high for everyone, including Parseghian. Still, he warned people at the start of spring practice that "it is far more difficult staying on top than it is getting there in the first place." That notion turned into a nightmare.

One by one, the wheels started falling off on the road to a repeat. Six players—three of them projected starters—were kicked out of school for a year after a serious dormitory infraction during the summer. Star running back Eric Penick broke his ankle in spring ball, and injuries to several other key players followed in the summer and early fall. Some were downright bizarre. Steve Quehl, a projected starter on the offensive line, was almost killed when the transmission of his truck blew up while he was working his summer job. Return specialist Tim Simon almost lost an eye during a freakish backyard incident. The luck of the Irish suddenly seemed to have turned bad.

Yet the Irish were still ranked No. 2 in the country when they squared off with Purdue in the third game of the season, having beaten both Georgia Tech and Northwestern. The Boilermakers, coached by former Parseghian assistant Alex Agase, jumped

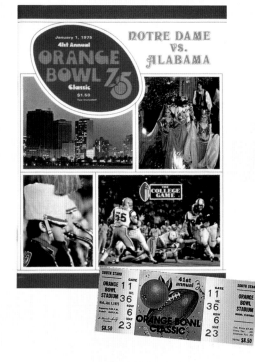

(left to right) Notre Dame's Reggie Barnett (14) runs with the ball after intercepting an Alabama pass during the fading minutes of the fourth quarter.
■ *Parseghian working the sideline in an earlier game. Over eleven seasons, his Notre Dame teams went 95–17–4, winning two national championships.*
■ *Game program and ticket from the 1975 Orange Bowl*

The Fighting Irish marching band performs.

on the Irish for twenty-four unanswered points in the first quarter and went on to a 31 to 20 victory. Parseghian sat in the small coaches' locker room at the Notre Dame Stadium, his hands in his face, as he sullenly answered reporters' questions. Although eight games remained, he knew his chances at a national title were diminished by the loss. His Irish rallied to win the next seven games but many were squeakers. After the Navy game, a 14 to 6 victory in which the Irish had trailed 6 to 0 early in the fourth quarter, Parseghian had decided to retire at season's end. Only his wife and brother knew his decision at that point. He tried to hide his feelings.

When the Irish rallied late again to beat Pittsburgh, he said of his players, "Two weeks ago after Navy, I told the team they were definitely causing my hair to turn gray. Today, I told them they were going to make me a replacement for Kojak." He was only laughing on the outside. He was taking sleeping pills and high–blood pressure medicine and feeling the weight of his decision to exit the profession he loved. Even so, his team headed into the regular season finale against USC with a 9–1 mark and an outside shot at the national title.

The Irish started out great against the Trojans at the Los Angeles Coliseum. They jumped out to a 24 to 0 lead late in the first half, only to have USC score

fifty-five unanswered points in just an eighteen-minute span. "What a disaster that was," Parseghian later said of what would become one of the most heartbreaking, devastating losses in Notre Dame football history. It almost made him reconsider his decision to resign. A few weeks later, though, he made the announcement that brought tears to the eyes of so many Irish faithful.

The odds seemed stacked against Notre Dame, facing undefeated and top-ranked Alabama in the Orange Bowl. To compound matters, linebacker Greg Collins, the team's leading tackler, sustained deep cuts to his knees that required several stitches after a motorcycle accident. On the offensive side, fullback Wayne Bullock, the leading rusher, was weakened by the flu. Needing all the help he could get, Parseghian still tried not to use his own departure from the game as a motivation.

"I told the players that they didn't owe me anything, but owed it to themselves to play a great game," he said. They did just that.

On touchdowns by a gutsy Bullock and Mark McLane, the Irish grabbed a 13 to 3 halftime lead. The defense, meanwhile, kept the Alabama offense at bay with Collins playing an outstanding game despite his injuries. "I don't know how he was able to play and not pop out his stitches," Parseghian said.

But the tide began to turn. On a fourth down play with 3:13 remaining in the game, Alabama quarterback Richard Todd hit Russ Schamun for a forty-eight–yard scoring play. A two-point conversion pass was also good, and the Crimson Tide were only behind by two, 13 to 11.

"I thought we had control of the game up to that point," Parseghian said. "But they completed that long pass that I thought our defensive back was going to intercept and, all of a sudden, we were in a dogfight."

Alabama got the ball back with less than two minutes to go, needing only a field goal to avenge the previous season's 24 to 23 loss to the Irish in the 1973 Sugar Bowl. But after Todd completed two passes, Notre Dame cornerback Reggie Barnett intercepted another on the Irish thirty-four with only 1:08 remaining.

"It was the biggest play I ever made," Barnett said.

"Before that interception, they probably thought they had their pickings with us with their passing," Parseghian said.

"But Reggie faked like he was going into deep coverage and then stopped and put himself in a perfect spot for the interception. A tremendous play."

It was a game-saver, and a great way for Parseghian to end his career. He was carried off the field as he

pumped his fist high into the air.

"As I reflect back on that night, I am so grateful with the way the players won that game, especially after all the injuries of that season and other disappointments," Parseghian recently said.

"I'll tell you, that was a much more pleasant way of leaving the game. And I will always appreciate that."

The "Era of Ara" was over. On that night, he did indeed stop the reign—even though Notre Dame fans wished it could go on and on.

(clockwise from top right) Alabama receiver Russ Schamun runs after catching a pass from Richard Todd. ■ Notre Dame senior halfback Al Samuel (24) gains ten yards on the first play of the fourth quarter for the Irish. ■ Samuel rushes with one of his ten carries before being stopped by the Crimson Tide defense.

Rudy! Rudy! Rudy!

Daniel "Rudy" Ruettiger was born in Illinois in 1948, the third of fourteen children. Like many of their neighbors in Joliet and in towns and cities across the Midwest, the Ruettigers were a blue-collar family. Daniel's parents grew up during the Great Depression and came of age during World War II. Settling down to raise their family, they taught their children to value the simple things, like hard work and the importance of setting goals.

Naturally, they also taught reverence for Notre Dame football.

Daniel explains, "Notre Dame football was their hope and inspiration. It was like a religion for the ethnic people coming back from the war. And that's what my Dad related to."

Today, it's Daniel Ruettiger that people from all walks of life relate to. Now known simply as "Rudy," his saga—depicted in the eponymous major motion picture—serves as inspiration to those who long to fulfill dreams of their own.

Rudy began his football career as an all-conference guard and linebacker at Joliet Catholic High School, and he's quick to point out today that he could never have attempted to play at Notre Dame if he hadn't been a good high school player, albeit at just 5 foot, 6 inches tall and 165 pounds. But good high school players in those days didn't automati-

cally plan on playing college football, especially for the always powerful Fighting Irish.

Coming out of high school, Rudy did what many young men at the time did. He joined the Navy. He worked in communications and spent part of his tour on a ship in the Mediterranean Sea. After receiving his discharge, he headed to South Bend and enrolled in Holy Cross Junior College. While at Holy Cross, Rudy learned he had a mild form of dyslexia, which may have affected his high school academic performance. "Holy Cross gave me a second chance," he now asserts, "and the GI Bill paid the bills." Rudy earned good grades and tried to get into Notre Dame. "I applied every semester and kept getting rejected." The closest he got to the field at Notre Dame Stadium was as a groundskeeper. He cut the grass.

Eventually, he was accepted into Notre Dame as a transfer student, and then he earned a spot on the scout football team (Joe Montana was on the same squad). But his initial acceptance as an athlete didn't come on the field. It came in the ring.

"I was a boxer at Notre Dame," Rudy recalls, "and I earned the players' respect by boxing against a football player. Eventually, I earned their respect in practice, but not right away."

(left to right) Linebacker Rudy Ruettiger (45) tackles Georgia Tech's Rudy Allen to finish the game for the Irish. ■ *November 8, 1975, game program and ticket*

(clockwise from bottom left) Ruettiger pictured in the Notre Dame yearbook ■ Sean Astin plays Rudy on the sidelines in the motion picture Rudy. ■ During the filming of Rudy, the real Ruettiger (right) met with actor Sean Astin (center).

But Rudy wanted to earn more than the players' respect. He wanted to earn a varsity letter, and to do that, he would have to play in at least one game for the Irish varsity squad.

At the end of his junior season, he was told by head coach Ara Parseghian that he would play as a senior and earn his letter.

But Parseghian left Notre Dame and was replaced by Dan Devine, who left a position as head coach of the Green Bay Packers to take over at Notre Dame. In the film Rudy, Devine is portrayed as the heavy, the guy who didn't want to let Rudy get in a game. And while acknowledging that such a portrayal was necessary as a cinematic device, Rudy is today sanguine regarding Devine's place in his story and asserts that the coach was not a bad guy at all.

"Dan Devine came in from the Packers and treated football as a business. He had no room for sympathy, it was his way of coaching." Rudy believes today that as a result of his efforts, Devine started to view walk-ons differently and that it was ultimately a good experience for the coach. Ruettiger also notes that Devine was hamstrung by NCAA rules that determined how many players could dress for each game.

Notre Dame was to play highly rated Georgia Tech in the final home game of Rudy's senior season, and he was not even scheduled to dress, much less play. For two years he had sacrificed his body against the starting offense, giving everything he had to help the regulars prepare for each game. Even if his coach wasn't ready to recognize his efforts, his teammates were.

What happened next ultimately became the best scene in the film. In the movie, senior after senior entered Devine's office and laid his jersey on the coach's desk, each asking that Rudy dress in his place. It was the ultimate recognition of their admiration for Rudy's effort. In reality, Daniel says, it was just a few key seniors who went to Devine, but the result was no less dramatic: Daniel Ruettiger was issued jersey number 45 and he dressed for the game.

The game was close, and with less than a minute to go, Rudy still had not played. Notre Dame had the ball and the lead late and was running out the clock. Ruettiger explains now that Devine wanted him to enter the game on offense, symbolically earning his letter. But Rudy was a linebacker and didn't want to go in on offense. Then, suddenly, Notre Dame scored and Devine put Rudy in on the kickoff team, allowing him to officially earn his letter.

With just twenty-two seconds left in the game, it was second and ten for Georgia Tech. As Georgia Tech quarterback Rudy Allen attempted one last desperate pass, Rudy Ruettiger seized the moment and lunged for Allen. Despite the dramatic call of the announcer portrayed in the movie, the real broadcasters, Mutual Radio's Al Wester and Don Criqui, never mentioned number 45, Daniel "Rudy" Ruettiger. "Rudy Allen drops to throw. They're going to get him. They do, back at the fourteen!" exclaimed Criqui. "Notre Dame's second line defensive unit swarms in to get Rudy Allen." The clock ticked off the final seconds and Notre Dame won by the lopsided score 24 to 3.

Although it was Notre Dame's "second line defensive unit" that got the credit, and the only "Rudy" mentioned by Criqui was Georgia Tech quarterback Rudy Allen, Daniel Ruettiger, his family, and his teammates who hoisted him off the field when the final gun sounded knew the true significance of the moment. It was a moment of personal triumph, the result of faith, perseverance, and sacrifice. In other words, it was a Notre Dame kind of moment.

After the game, Rudy saw his father. It was the only time he ever saw his dad get emotional. "I'm very proud of you, son," his father said.

Today, Daniel Ruettiger maintains a good relationship with the Notre Dame football program. He received a degree in sociology from the university and credits his time there with his success in life. That success includes the hit film that bears his name and tells his story.

Rudy's name has become ubiquitous with the player or person who maximizes his accomplishments through guts, hard work, and determination. He is now the head of Rudy International and an in-demand motivational speaker. His message is simple. "It's a message of hope and inspiration," he says. "I try to inspire people to do better and to realize their dreams."

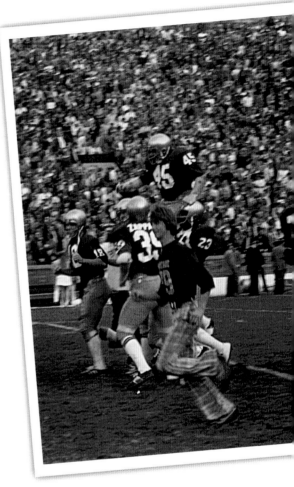

After playing in his first college game, Rudy is carried on the shoulders of his teammates.

Irish Beat Campbell and Texas in the 1978 Cotton Bowl

"I think we are going to beat them soundly," Irish linebacker Bob Golic told the press just days before the 1978 Cotton Bowl. "In my opinion, it won't be a squeaker." The angry eyes of Texas were suddenly upon Golic and his Irish teammates.

The Irish, ranked fifth in the country, were getting ready to play the No. 1 Longhorns, led by Heisman Trophy winner Earl Campbell and Outland Trophy recipient Brad Shearer. And Golic, Notre Dame's leading tackler, sounded as if he were taunting, or at least teasing, the proud Texans. Coach Dan Devine quickly made it clear to the free-spirited Golic that he didn't want to hear another word out of him like that. Yet deep down, most of the Irish players felt the same kind of confidence going into what would become the national championship game.

After starting off the season ranked No. 1, Notre Dame had struggled to a 19 to 9 victory over Pittsburgh in the opener before being upset by Ole Miss, 20 to 13. Then it took the off-the-bench heroics of junior third-string quarterback Joe Montana to pull out a 31 to 24 victory at Purdue. The come-from-behind victory against the Boilermakers and Montana in the starting lineup seemed to give the Irish the lift their season needed. Notre Dame went on to win their next eight games, including an emotional 49 to 19 victory over USC in which the Irish unveiled green jerseys just before kickoff.

Texas, meanwhile, was coming off a storybook regular season under first-year coach Fred Akers. The Longhorns had rebounded from a 5–5–1 campaign in 1976 to finish the '77 regular season as the only undefeated major-college team. Along the way, they had handed both Oklahoma and Arkansas their only defeats of the season. And, of course, they had the great running back Earl Campbell. "I was talking to [Oklahoma coaching legend] Bud Wilkinson," Devine said before the game, "and he said he'd never seen a back that big with that much speed. Or was it a back with that much speed who was that big?"

This particular Irish defense, which sometimes played second fiddle to Montana's emergence in the headlines, may have been one of the best Irish defenses ever. No less than eight of the starters would later play in the NFL, including future All-Pros Ross Browner and Golic. They were also healthy. "We won't have any excuses," said Devine on the eve of the game. Then he laughed and joked, "Maybe we should look around for some."

(left to right) Notre Dame halfback Terry Eurick charges through the Longhorn defense. ■ *Brothers Ross and Jim Browner team up to bring down a Longhorn runner.* ■ *Game program and ticket from the 1978 Cotton Bowl*

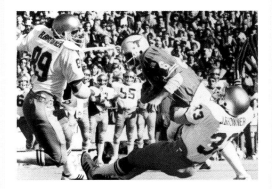

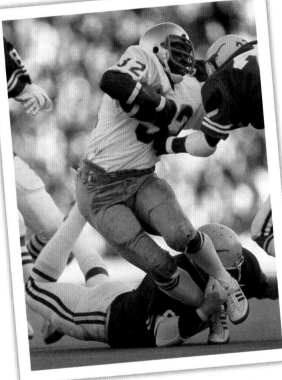

The Irish defenders ended up looking for loose balls instead. They were devastating—forcing three fumbles and grabbing three interceptions on the chilly January afternoon in front of 76,701 in the stands, the largest Cotton Bowl crowd in history. The game was televised nationally on CBS. Paul Alexander, former Irish Heisman winner Paul Hornung, and Lindsey Nelson watched from their booth as Notre Dame set the tone for the game early in the first quarter. It was third and one at the forty-five–yard line when Browner and Golic sandwiched Texas quarterback Randy McEachern as he attempted to pitch the ball to Campbell. "There's the pitch and it's loose!" exclaimed Nelson. "The scramble is on," he cried, as Notre Dame players and officials began waiving their arms indicating the turnover. "Notre Dame has recovered it at the thirty-two–yard line!" Browner recovered the ball to set up a forty-seven–yard field goal by Irish kicker Dave Reeve.

Then, after Texas knotted the score at three, strong safety Jim Browner, Ross's little brother, recovered another fumble. Irish back Terry Eurick scored four plays later. The Irish defensive pressure continued. Willie Fry came up with another first-half fumble and Doug Becker intercepted a pass to set up other scoring drives.

Montana drove the Irish to within seventeen yards of the end zone with 7:28 left in the second quarter. "Montana back now. Montana's throwing!" exclaimed Lindsey Nelson, "and it's in the end zone! Touchdown Vagas Ferguson!…Touchdown Notre Dame!" Ferguson caught a spectacular seventeen-yard touchdown pass from Montana. "After Vagas caught his touchdown pass, I was the first one to get to him," tight end Ken MacAfee said. "He was just sitting there in the end zone saying 'I can't believe I caught that.' I think that summed up how we all felt about the game." The field goal gave the Irish a halftime lead of 24 to 10.

The rout was on in the second half as both Steve Heimkreiter and Randy Harrison picked off McEachern passes, and Vagas Ferguson added two more unanswered touchdowns. The six turnovers that the Irish defense forced for the day made it easy on the offense. They scored after five of those turnovers on drives of just twenty-seven, thirty-five, twenty, twenty-nine, and fifty yards. Although Montana didn't have one of his better days passing (just ten of twenty-five for 111 yards), the Irish backs more than made up for it. Fullback Jerome Heavens totaled 101 yards on twenty-two carries, and Ferguson ran for exactly one hundred yards on twenty-one carries and three touchdowns. When time expired, the Irish were on the Texas one-yard line and could have scored again, but contented themselves with a final score of Notre Dame 38, Texas 10. The Texas stands were empty.

Although the Notre Dame offense made the most of its opportunities, most would agree that the defense carried the day in Big D. The Irish defense bottled up Campbell. Although he did lead all rushers with 116 yards, it took him twenty-nine carries with his longest run only eighteen yards. The Heisman winner ran hard but took plenty of hard knocks. Near the end of the game, he had to be helped off the field after one of many jarring tackles. "We call that our corral defense," said Notre Dame defensive coordinator Joe Yonto, whose players held the Longhorns offense to 291 yards.

The lopsided victory helped catapult the Irish into first place in both major polls for the national championship. A few other teams with 11–1 marks—including Alabama, Arkansas, and even Texas—thought they might have gotten more consideration. No. 3 Alabama had beat up on Ohio

(top to bottom) Irish defensive end Ross Browner recovers a fumble in the first quarter. ■ Notre Dame halfback Vagas Ferguson rushed for one hundred yards and three touchdowns in the game.

State, 35 to 6, in the Sugar Bowl and No. 6 Arkansas had humbled No. 2 Oklahoma, 31 to 6, in the Orange Bowl.

Ironically, the first-year Arkansas coach, whose team's effort helped the Irish win the title, would later win a national championship at Notre Dame himself. But after the 1977–78 bowls, Lou Holtz had mixed feelings about the voting. "I have no problem justifying Notre Dame as No. 1," Lou reasoned, "but I have a problem justifying why Arkansas and Alabama aren't No. 1 along with them."

Dan Devine was as relieved as he was elated. During an unguarded moment the previous spring, the Notre Dame coach had said, "If we don't win with these players, we're all in trouble." But after his team lost to Ole Miss in the season's second game, "Dump Devine" stickers started to show up around the campus. That campaign quickly ended as the Irish marched on to ten straight victories. In fact, the only person who wanted to pull Devine's chain a little after the 1978 Cotton Bowl was the game's defensive MVP. That was Bob Golic, who also turned out to be a pretty fair pigskin prognosticator.

"I just had to remind Coach," the big-smiling line-backer said, referring to his pregame promise of an Irish victory, "that I was right all along."

(clockwise from top right) Quarterback Joe Montana prepares to hand off. ■ While Montana begins to smile, coach Dan Devine turns and hugs one of his players as the last seconds tick away in the '78 Cotton Bowl. ■ Irish back Terry Eurick (40) heads for the end zone.

Montana's Chicken Soup Heroics

They called him Notre Dame's Comeback Kid. But this time, Joe Montana wasn't coming back. Or so they thought. At halftime of the 1979 Cotton Bowl, the senior quarterback was in bad shape, suffering from a pesky flu bug and facing blizzard-like conditions that lowered Dallas's temperature to sixteen degrees and plummeted the windchill factor to ten below zero. In front of a shivering crowd of 32,500 and a national television audience watching on CBS, Houston was in the lead, 20 to 12. The Fighting Irish needed Montana "to shake down the thunder" in the second half. Instead, he sat in the locker room at the intermission, shaking uncontrollably.

"We were told that Joe wasn't coming back in the second half and we thought it was over," said Irish center Dave Huffman. What followed was vintage Montana with a little luck—and cluck—thrown in. Houston owned a seemingly insurmountable 34 to 12 lead with just over seven minutes to play, only to have Notre Dame, with Montana back at the helm, pull off the greatest comeback victory in school history.

"The official report from the team physician is that he has the chills," said CBS color commentator Frank Glieber, bringing broadcast boothmates Lindsey Nelson and Paul Hornung, and a national viewing audience, up to date on Montana's health. "His body temperature is below normal. They're

giving him warm fluids, and he may be back before the end of the game. He said it's kind of like the start of the flu."

Notre Dame team doctor Les Bodnar, an orthopedic surgeon by trade, ended up having the right recipe for victory in his bag. Staying behind in the locker room with Montana after the half, Bodnar pulled out a packet of chicken soup he had received as a Christmas stocking stuffer from one of his daughters. He warmed the soup over a Bunsen burner and spoon-fed Montana until the senior quarterback's body temperature was back to normal.

What followed was anything but normal. Montana returned late in the third quarter. Receiver Kris Haines knew there was hope. "When Joe came back to the field, I started thinking this was a fairy tale," said Montana's buddy and favorite receiver. "I thought how he had done it so many times before. This time, though, it had to be a miracle."

Montana may have been warmed up from the soup, but he returned with no sign of a hot hand. After a mediocre first half (six of fifteen passing and two interceptions), Montana completed just one of his first eleven passes in the second half and threw his third interception. The Irish already had lost linebacker Bob Golic and safety Joe Restic, the team's

(left to right) Notre Dame quarterback Joe Montana runs out of the arms of Houston's Fred Snell during the game's decisive final drive. ■ Game program and ticket from the 1979 Cotton Bowl

defensive leaders, to injuries. And Montana looked just plain lost.

But an Irish storm was about to erupt as Tony Belden blocked a Houston punt and fellow freshman Steve Cichy returned it thirty-three yards for a touchdown with 7:25 remaining. Montana followed with a two-point conversion pass to Vagas Ferguson to cut the deficit to 34 to 20. Getting the ball back quickly, Montana led the Irish on a sixty-one–yard, five-play drive, going the last two yards himself. Then he hit Haines for the two-point conversion to make it 34 to 28, with 4:15 remaining.

Again the Irish got the ball back quickly, but this time Montana fumbled. Houston couldn't move the ball far, though, and faced fourth down. Houston coaches decided to go for the first down from their own twenty-nine instead of punting into a stiff wind. Their plan backfired when defensive linemen Joe Gramke and Mike Calhoun stuffed Houston back Emmett King for no gain. The Irish

had the ball with twenty-eight seconds remaining and twenty-nine yards to go. Montana first scrambled for eleven yards, then hit Haines again on a ten-yard sideline pattern.

Six seconds were now left with the ball on the Houston eight. Offensive coordinator Merv Johnson turned to head coach Dan Devine and said, "Do you want to get in two quick plays or one sure one?" Devine opted for the two. "But the first play had to be something quick," the coach later said, "and the only plays we have like that with a three-step drop are '91'—a quick turnout by the wide receivers—or '92'—a quick slant by both." Devine gave Montana the choice of the two. He picked '91.' "If I see it's not there, I'm supposed to get rid of the ball right away," Montana said after the game.

When Montana saw that Haines was closely covered, he tossed it out of harm's way to allow enough time for another chance. All but the last two seconds had clicked off the clock. Montana remembered what Devine had told him during the timeout, "If your first pass is incomplete, you call what is most comfortable to you."

(clockwise from bottom left) Safety Jim Browner brings down a Houston runner. ■ *Montana hands off to fullback Pete Pallas.* ■ *An ailing Montana completed only six of fifteen passes in the first half.*

The future Hall of Famer from Monongahela, Pennsylvania, looked around the huddle and then asked Haines if he could beat his man. Haines said he could. Montana smiled. "Let's do it. OK, guys same play." "Then he took his finger and showed how Kris was going to go in the corner again," tailback Vagas Ferguson recalled.

Despite the awful conditions and only a few thousand people still in the stands, it was a picture-perfect spot for Montana and his last-second heroics. His body may have shaken earlier, but his voice never did—not even under the everything-on-the-line circumstances. Before Montana took his spot behind Huffman, he looked over at the Irish bench and nodded, letting them know it would be the same play, '91.'

Montana and Haines had worked endless hours with one another on such plays the previous summer, trying to perfect their timing. They were ready for all that preparation to pay off. "Two seconds left to play. The clock will start on the snap," Lindsey Nelson told the viewing audience, "Houston 34, Notre Dame 28." There was no time showing on the clock after Montana rolled to his right. "Montana throwing!" He found a diving Haines in the corner of the end zone.

"And it's a touchdown! A touchdown taken at the corner!" shouted Nelson. "Unbelievable finish!" added Hornung, "Houston on top 34 to 12 and now it's all tied up!" The Irish sidelines went wild and Montana was mobbed by his teammates. "What a finish!…I've never seen anything like it!" proclaimed Paul Hornung, "Notre Dame completely came back in the fourth quarter to win it by one!" But not until Joe Unis, a Dallas native, had to kick the extra point twice due to an offsides call after his first successful kick. But the Irish had their almost unbelievable 35 to 34 victory, featuring a twenty-three–point comeback in less than eight minutes. The defense may have set the stage in the final minutes, but it was Montana again who had saved the day. "Joe had to throw that last pass low and inside," Haines said, "and he threw it right where it had to be. It was so clutch."

The victory was the six-hundredth in Notre Dame history and the greatest on a long list of great comebacks. The Comeback Kid saw to that. Montana proved to have the perfect recipe—the indomitable Notre Dame spirit and old-fashioned chicken soup—to fuel Notre Dame to victory on a bone-chilling but thrilling day.

(left to right) Montana prepares to pass. ■ *Irish players Dave Huffman (56) and Kris Haines (82) celebrate the incredible come-from-behind victory.*

Harry O' Gets the Call

When Notre Dame and Michigan meet on the football field, there is something special in the air. And on those Saturdays, if the air stands still, it can be even more special, like it was on September 20, 1980, during one of the most thrilling finishes in a series that dates back to 1887.

In the game's closing seconds, with fifty-one yards to the crossbar and a gusting fifteen-mile-an-hour wind, Harry Oliver took his place in Irish lore.

The Irish had grabbed an early 14 to 0 lead, but by late in the third quarter the Wolverines were out front 21 to 14. With 1:03 left in the third quarter, Notre Dame cornerback John Krimm dashed forty-nine yards for a touchdown after intercepting a John Wangler pass intended for Michigan All-American Anthony Carter. The Irish hoped to tie the game with the extra point kick from Harry Oliver, but it wasn't to be. Despite kicking with the

wind, Oliver missed the extra point and the frustrated Irish trailed 21 to 20.

A seventy-four–yard drive capped by a four-yard scoring run by Phil Carter gave Notre Dame a 26 to 21 lead late in the fourth quarter. The Irish failed on their two-point conversion attempt. Michigan charged back with their own long touchdown drive, this one seventy-eight yards. But they too missed on a two-point conversion, leaving them in the lead by the razor-thin margin of 27 to 26.

Now with just twenty seconds left in the game, Notre Dame was at its own twenty with the wind in its face, behind freshman quarterback Blair Kiel. Kiel moved the Irish forward, benefiting from a controversial pass interference call, then getting to the Michigan thirty-nine after a nine-yard pass to Phil Carter. Now, it was fourth and one for Notre Dame, with just nine seconds left and no time-outs remaining. In order to move the ball even closer for Harry Oliver, Kiel and Devine would need to throw to a receiver on a sideline pattern.

"Well, it's miracle time for Notre Dame," announced Tony Roberts and Al Wester, calling the game for Mutual Radio. "Kiel, waiting for the snap under center…looks, barks out the count…long count by Kiel…back to throw, takes the snap…has the time, looking, throws…sideline…Hunter made the catch!"

(left to right) Harry Oliver kicks the game-winning field goal as a Michigan defender dives to block. ■ *Pete Holohan (31) of Notre Dame catches a touchdown pass.* ■ *September 10, 1980, game program and ticket*

(left to right) Michigan All-American Anthony Carter is tackled at the sideline. ■ Late in the third quarter, Notre Dame's John Krimm intercepted Wangler's pass and returned it forty-nine yards for a touchdown. ■ Harry Oliver kicks an extra point.

Kiel completed a five-yard toss to Tony Hunter, moving the ball up to the Michigan thirty-four.

Just four seconds remained, and coach Dan Devine called for Oliver. "He didn't say much," Oliver recalled. "I would always stand up close to him and wait until I heard, '*Field goal!*' and run out. That's the only thing I remember him saying." He remembered the wind more clearly. "I felt a rush of wind in my face when I ran out there."

Just before setting down his tee, Oliver heard his holder, former high school teammate Tim Koegel, prepare him for the worst. "Tim asked me if I was ready and I said, 'Sure, why?'" Oliver explained.

"Because I have a better chance of running this thing in than you do of kicking in there," Koegel responded. Koegel, of course, turned into a better quarterback than a prophet. "Just kick the hell out of it," Koegel advised, "and kick it straight." Oliver had his doubts, and his performance on the day didn't bode well for Irish hopes.

He already had missed an extra point earlier, which was why the Irish trailed 27 to 26 instead of being tied. "I hated to think we were going to lose because

of me," Oliver said. "So I spent that last drive getting myself mentally and physically ready for the challenge. I just hoped I would get the chance."

"Before the game, I remember kicking sixty-five–yard field goals when I had the wind at my back. But now it was back in my face. Honestly, I didn't know if I could do it. But I thought if I kept it low because of the wind, it had a chance," he said. "Everyone asks me if the wind actually stopped before the kick. Put it this way: if it didn't, I didn't have a prayer." But prayer would be mentioned later as a guess for why the wind stopped. It was as if Mother Nature got the memo from Touchdown Jesus just in time. Suddenly it was still. And Oliver was ready.

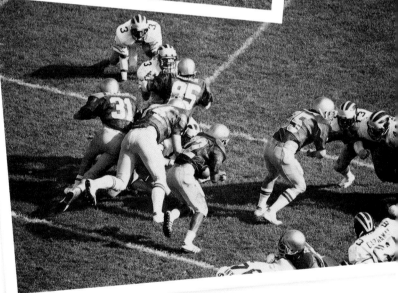

"This is it. Harry O' gets the call!" announced Roberts. "The ball to be spotted down by Koegel at the forty-one. A fifty-one–yard boot! This is the ballgame!" Oliver stepped his usual two steps back and two steps over. Long-snapper Bill Siewe made a perfect snap. Koegel placed a perfect hold. And Oliver swung his left leg through with the grace of a good golf swing.

Roberts called the critical moment, "The kick is up and it is…*good! good!* He made it! A fifty-one–yard field goal by Harry Oliver! And Notre Dame has won it 29 to 27 as time runs out!" Bedlam erupted in Notre Dame Stadium. Irish players flooded the field. And then Al Wester voiced an observation, tacitly invoking the notion of divine intervention. His comment not only underscored the miraculous kick, but enshrined it in Notre Dame lore, "He kicked it into the wind! I watched the flags. Just as he got ready to kick, believe it or not, those flags went limp! The wind had shifted. His kick was right there! Just there in time! Notre Dame with a miracle win as the clock runs out!" Under the mass of happy humanity somewhere was Oliver, whose smile was wider than his face mask.

Notre Dame had toppled Michigan on a magical kick by the man they called "Harry O'." "I didn't even see it go through the goalposts," he said. "You could just feel it." In the locker room after the game, Oliver had a better view than most of his teammates because he was sitting on their shoulders.

After Father James Riehle blessed the victory, Oliver found Devine, the man who took a chance on him with a scholarship. "I whispered to him, 'Coach, this was for you because you gave me a chance,'" Oliver said. Years later, his booming boot still resonates with Irish fans who meet up with Oliver. "You know," he said later, "it still comes up almost every day in conversation."

(left to right) Michigan's Craig Dunaway hauls in a touchdown pass. ■ Quarterback Blair Kiel throws over a defender. ■ Notre Dame halfback Phil Carter scores on a four-yard run to give the Irish a 26 to 21 lead late in the fourth quarter.

Irish Upset No. 1 Pitt

In one of the most improbable intersections of preparation and opportunity, a spirited man whose career had been coaching football to teenagers at a Catholic high school in Ohio was tapped for the most prestigious job in his sport—because he built a reputation for coaching young men in the game of life as well.

After watching him build Cincinnati Moeller High School into a national prep powerhouse, Notre Dame stunned pundits and fans by naming the enthusiastic, sometimes naïve, optimistic charmer, Gerry Faust, its head football coach to succeed Dan Devine.

At a place where the spotlight is as blinding as any program in the land, no Irish head man received more hype, buildup, and scrutiny than Faust in his inaugural season in '81. Faust's first collegiate game—a win over LSU that vaulted Notre Dame to No. 1 in the polls—gave rise to high hopes for this humble, folksy, and tireless worker. But the fairy tale hit a brick wall. A disappointing 5–6 season left many true believers doubting Faust's magic.

So in the autumn of 1982, Faust's mission was to silence his critics and please the team's loyal followers. After a lifetime on the sidelines, he had his dream job. Now he needed a dream season.

The season featuring college football's who's who on the schedule began in earnest. There were consecutive wins, first over Michigan in a first-ever night game at Notre Dame Stadium, and then against intrastate rival Purdue. Then it was a dangerous yet victorious road trip to Michigan State, followed by an Irish win over juggernaut Miami thanks to last-second dramatics by the Irish. But a surprise home loss to Arizona and a stunning tie with the lowly Oregon Ducks before a record crowd in Eugene left the Irish wobbly, and their national championship aspirations all but gone.

A win over Navy helped stop the bleeding, but it was going to take a whole lot more to convince people Gerry Faust was up to this challenge.

Their task could hardly be more daunting, as the Irish faced a record crowd in Pitt Stadium, a No. 1–ranked Pitt Panthers crew, and one of the game's most prolific passers in quarterback Dan Marino.

"We go into Pittsburgh," said defensive tackle Mike Golic, "Dan Marino is a senior. Their offensive line

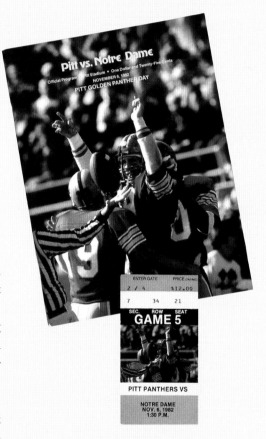

(left to right) Tailback Allen Pinkett runs seventy-six yards for a crucial Irish score in the fourth quarter. ■ *A potential touchdown pass to Julius Dawkins is batted away by Irish defender Chris Braun.* ■ *November 6, 1982, game program and ticket*

has [future NFL stars] Bill Fralic and Jimbo Covert. They're ranked No. 1—and we're not ranked at all."

Maybe the critics were right. Maybe Gerry Faust didn't belong. Maybe the college ranks were too high a bar for him to clear. Maybe putting a man with no coaching experience above the high school level had disaster written all over it.

(top to bottom) Blair Kiel completes a nine-yard pass to Mike Haywood in the first quarter. ■ Notre Dame's Phil Carter aims upfield, but is stopped by Pitt's Al Wenglikowski.

But Faust wasn't ready to admit to any of that. He designed a pregame speech that played up two of the most popular themes in Irish football legend: sacrifice and upsets. First, Faust cited each game in which Notre Dame had knocked off a No. 1–ranked opponent, challenging his troops to join the school's fraternity of giant-killers. Next, he let them know their No. 1 fan—a young man from South Bend confined to his wheelchair by cerebral palsy—had made the trip that morning, by bus and by himself, just to see the team he loved add another thrilling chapter to its history of upsets.

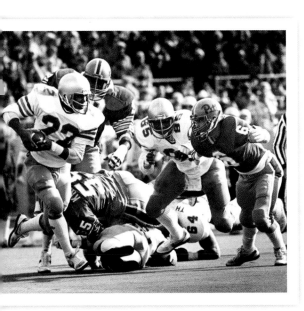

From the opening kickoff, fans got their money's worth of theater and dramatics. The Panthers drew first blood, and they did so early. Marino engineered a scoring drive on Pitt's very first possession as they took a 3 to 0 lead that stood the entire first quarter. Pitt opened the second quarter the same way, marching down the field and threatening with first and goal from the Notre Dame four-yard line.

But a goal line stance for the Irish defense netted Pitt merely a field goal—meaning even with all Marino's firepower, Notre Dame was only a touchdown away from taking the lead on the nation's top-ranked team.

The Irish coaching staff had prepared their charges extremely well, formulating daring game plans both offensively and defensively. Now, with some momentum on their side, they occupied the field with a "hold nothing back" attitude. When the Panthers shanked a punt deep in their own territory, Notre Dame's fortunate field position resulted in a field goal. When the Panthers fumbled on their next possession, Irish quarterback Blair Kiel and company looked to capitalize. The offense produced its first lead less than a minute later thanks to big plays by Allen Pinkett and Larry Moriarty. The Irish took a surprising 10 to 6 lead into halftime.

Nearly the entire third quarter went scoreless, until Marino constructed an almost nine-minute touchdown drive the length of the field to put Pitt ahead 13 to 10.

And so the fourth quarter began, crunch time for the Irish and Faust. Notre Dame's defense had been worn down. Pitt's ninety-eight–yard drive had energized the home crowd. After a year and a half of the college football world questioning whether Gerry Faust belonged in the big leagues, there would never be a better opportunity to find out.

The Notre Dame faithful in the stadium, as well as those listening to Mutual Radio's Tony Roberts and Al Wester, were hoping for some of the legendary Irish luck. It came when Faust decided to unleash a more daring game plan in the first drive of the quarter. "First down and ten for the Irish at the forty-five–yard line. Down by three, 13 to 10," said Roberts as he watched Notre Dame line up.

Just short of midfield, Kiel pitched right to halfback Phil Carter, who appeared to start a run-of-the-mill sweep. But Carter suddenly stopped. To the surprise of the Pitt defense, he pitched back to Kiel. "Carter—flea-flicker back to Kiel!" said Roberts in a voice that rose with excitement at every word. "Kiel looking. Throwing!" Kiel threw a wobbling fifty-five–yard toss to flanker Joe Howard. "Joe Howard down the field! Gets the ball!" Wide open at the seven, Howard cradled the ball and entered the end zone untouched.

"Touchdown!" shouted Roberts. The Irish fans in the stadium erupted and so did Wester, "What a play! What a play, the old 'flea-flicker'…Kiel has just thrown his longest pass of the year! He was behind his man a good five yards, little Joe Howard grabbed it at the five, waltzes in, touchdown! The Irish are back in front 16 to 13!"

"It wasn't a perfect pass," Kiel later said, "but I'm glad that ball was a little wobbly or I might have thrown it too deep." A successful extra point pushed the Irish lead to 17 to 13.

"It was a hell of a play," said Pitt defensive lineman Bill Dukovich. "They disguised it well. It looked like a sweep. I came up. But you stay deep. There's no excuse." Not ready to roll over, Marino went to work and used short tosses to get his team within range of what would be a successful field goal. Only a point separated the two squads.

But then the kind of break that busts tight games open happened. Pitt's wide receiver Johnny Dawkins took a crackling Mike Larkin hit, and Notre Dame's John Mosley grabbed his fumble. With a little more than eight minutes remaining in the game, the Irish were first and ten at their own twenty-four–yard line. Kiel launched a quick pass to Joe Howard. But Howard was double-covered by Pittsburgh's Dukovich and Troy Hill and the ball sailed over his head. Now it was second and ten for Notre Dame, and Pinkett was determined to keep the lead the flea-flicker had given them.

Mutual's Tony Roberts called it, "In motion, Tony Hunter is wide out to the left side. Hand off. Pinkett, off to left side. At the twenty-five! Get to the thirty! To the thirty-five! To the forty!" shouted Roberts, thrilled by what he was witnessing. "To the forty-five! To the fifty! He may go all the way! He's going to win the race! He's at the twenty, the ten!"

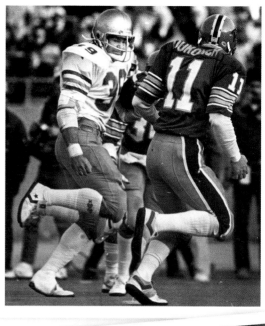

Pinkett weaved through five Panther defenders and raced seventy-six yards to the end zone. "Touchdown Notre Dame!" exclaimed Roberts. "Absolutely, the most stunning run that I have seen a Notre Dame running back turn in, in the last ten years!" observed Al Wester. Almost in unison, a wall of Irish coaches, trainers, and players on the sidelines jumped up as they witnessed what had happened.

"It was a sprint-draw play in which I have the option to go out or cut across," said Pinkett. "I saw two guys collapsing on me, but saw a little bubble between them. I just decided to get through there as quickly as I possibly could."

Despite 8:09 showing on the clock in the fourth quarter, the Panthers' fate was sealed. The Irish never relinquished the lead—and even added to it, finishing off the Panthers 31 to 16. "We didn't just beat them," said Golic, "we crushed them on their home field." "This is the biggest win I've ever experienced in my career," said Irish linebacker Mark Zavagnin. "I'll remember this forever," echoed senior offensive lineman Tom Thayer. "31 to 16…I'll never forget that score."

Two celebrations awaited the squad. The first, in a jubilant locker room, where the prophetic Faust presented South Bend superfan Keith Penrod the game ball; the second, in South Bend and on famed Notre Dame Avenue, where thousands of students stood shoulder to shoulder during an impromptu pep rally. Faust had the pleasure of enjoying his first "welcome home" since his tenure began. "I could see the tears in his eyes as the bus crawled through the cheering students," said Moriarty. "He's a great man to be around, because he's so happy. Everybody wants to see him succeed because he loves Notre Dame so much and works so hard."

For one night, it was Faust's Notre Dame.

(top to bottom) Larry Moriarty gains big yardage in the fourth quarter to set up a final Notre Dame touchdown. ■ A key turnover in the game was Julius Dawkins' fumble, which was recovered by Notre Dame's Mike Larkin.

Notre Dame Beats Miami in 1988

While not the longest running, nor the most significant of Notre Dame football matchups, the Miami Hurricanes became as bitter a rival in the 1980s as any at Notre Dame. In fact, the rivalry became so fierce that, citing "the interest of the schools, the students, and collegiate sports," officials at both schools ended the annual game in 1990.

In their four previous meetings, Miami had dominated the Irish by a collective margin of 133 to 20, including a 58 to 7 drubbing in 1985. In that game, Miami's infamous coach, Jimmy Johnson, poured on offensive scoring well into the fourth quarter. The humiliating, blow-out game was the last in head coach Gerry Faust's Notre Dame career. Avenging that loss was in the hearts and minds of Notre Dame students, fans, and players alike as the Hurricanes came to South Bend in October 1988. Even as early as the school year before the

matchup, a student magazine on campus printed a poster of Jimmy Johnson announcing, "Avoid the Rush, Hate Miami Early. Only 198 Days Left!"

By the week of the anticipated game, signs proclaiming "Remember 58–7" and more distasteful statements referring to Miami's notorious football program and their coach hung from dorm rooms across campus. Miami's sports department, and even Jimmy Johnson's home, were flooded with phone calls and postcards from overzealous Irish fans. Pregame hype had grown to such an unprecedented height that the university, Coach Lou Holtz, and the team captains all made public requests in the days before the game for the students and fans to express their excitement about the matchup in more "positive" ways.

By gameday, young entrepreneurs were adding fuel to the pregame fire, selling the latest in anti-Miami T-shirt propaganda to tens of thousands of fans. Although officially frowned upon by the university, Notre Dame fans can still be spotted from time to time wearing the most popular of those '88 Miami game T-shirts, "Catholics vs. Convicts—Unfinished Business."

(left to right) Pat Terrell (15) leaps to bat the ball away from Miami's Leonard Conley (28) and save the game for Notre Dame. ■ The Rocket blasts past the Miami bench on his way to the end zone. ■ October 15, 1988, game program and ticket

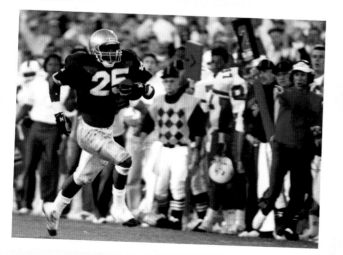

The packed Stepan Center crowd of players and fans roared with excitement.

Unlike typical autumn days in South Bend, this October afternoon seemed more like Florida, with the sun shining brightly and temperatures reaching the mid-70s. The weather was perfect for the thousands of Notre Dame fans who had been eating, drinking, and celebrating at tailgate parties throughout the stadium parking lots for days leading up to gameday. At Notre Dame, tailgate festivities have been perfected, and the days leading up to this historic Notre Dame–Miami matchup were no exception. By game time, tickets were being scalped outside the stadium for up to $1,000 apiece.

Amid all of the hype and heat, it wasn't surprising that the afternoon began with an all-out skirmish between the teams at the entrance of the stadium tunnel during warm-ups. By kickoff, the Irish players and the roaring

(top to bottom) Quarterback Tony Rice (9) celebrates a touchdown.
■ *Lou Holtz and Jimmy Johnson meet on the field before the game.*
■ *Notre Dame's Pat Terrell runs with an interception.*

Coming into South Bend, Miami was ranked No. 1. They were defending national champions and had won thirty-six regular season games in a row, including twenty straight road games. Holtz, now in his third year as head coach, needed to get everything he could out of the No. 4 Irish that day. At the student pep rally the night before the big game, using motivational tactics that Knute Rockne himself would be proud of, Holtz surprisingly and boldly guaranteed an Irish victory against Miami.

crowd of 59,075 were ready to witness one of the most hard-fought, back-and-forth games in Notre Dame history. The thrilling game would feature a blocked field goal, a foiled fake punt, four interceptions, five lost fumbles, and a controversial sixth.

Early in the second quarter, Pat Terrell intercepted a pass by Miami's Steve Walsh and returned it for a touchdown to give the Irish a 21 to 7 lead. At the time, Terrell may have thought his touchdown run was his best play of the day. He admits now that history has convinced him otherwise.

The Hurricanes were not about to leave South Bend without making a game of it. Scoring on two of Steve Walsh's three touchdown passes of the game (he would finish the game a career high thirty-one of fifty for 424 yards), the determined Hurricanes tied the score as the first half ended.

Notre Dame stormed out of the locker room for the second half, invigorated by a memorable motivational speech. As Notre Dame teams do, the offense and the defense spent halftime in the locker room on opposite sides of a two-sided blackboard. As the offensive players wound up their discussion about their second half game plan, the Notre Dame defensive players were ranting and raving about their intentions for the second half. Suddenly, with

all the fierce emotion of the moment, a defensive coach's fist came blasting through and shattered the blackboard, to the surprise and excitement of all.

The Irish scored ten unanswered points in the third quarter behind senior quarterback Tony Rice, Tony Brooks, and stars Ricky Watters, Florida-native Derek Brown, Pat Eilers, and diminutive kicker Reggie Ho. Defensive lineman Jeff Alm also added a skyscraping interception in a third quarter dominated by the Irish. And defensive end Frank Stams continued to play like a champion. Later calling the day "absolutely perfect," Stams physically and emotionally led the Notre Dame defense, sacking the previously un-sacked Walsh, causing mayhem by putting backfield pressure on the Hurricanes, tipping the pass Terrell intercepted for a touchdown, causing two Miami fumbles, and recovering another.

Miami stormed back in the fourth quarter behind a Carlos Huerta field goal, and with five minutes to play, the Hurricanes nearly tied it with a would-be touchdown that was ruled a fumble, yet remains a source of controversy to this day. The game-saving hit to cause the fumble was made by Notre Dame's punishing Michael Stonebreaker, and recovered by

(left to right) Offensive guard Tim Grunhard (75) celebrates a touchdown with his teammates. ■ The Notre Dame defense brings down Miami quarterback Steve Walsh.

(top to bottom) Notre Dame's offensive onslaught was aided by the efforts of kicker Reggie Ho (2). ■ Terrell leaps to bat down the potential game-winning two-point conversion pass from Walsh.

team cocaptain George Streeter. The controversy over whether Cleveland Gary broke the plane of the goal line before taking the hit from Stonebreaker will always be a sore spot for Miami fans.

The Hurricanes were still down by seven points and regained the ball, moving it to the Notre Dame eleven. It was fourth down and six, fifty-one seconds left to play when, like they had done so many times before (including an amazing comeback victory against Michigan just four weeks earlier), Miami came through in the clutch. Quarterback Steve Walsh hit Andre Brown with an "over the shoulder," a fade pattern in the end zone, putting the Hurricanes within one point of the Irish. What would Jimmy Johnson do now? Go for one point and the tie, letting the polls decide his fate? Go for the two-pointer and the win, but risk a loss? Johnson would later explain without regret, "We always play to win."

With the cool confidence of a team sure of its destiny, and amid the loudest crowd in Notre Dame history, registering at 110 decibels on the sideline, the Irish approached the line of scrimmage with just forty-five seconds left. Across the line of scrimmage was the most successful, toughest, fastest team in college football. They knew what they had to do. For a moment, it seemed as if the echoes of football seasons past and a parade of Irish ghosts joined Notre Dame faithful everywhere, rallying their team for one last play as Steve Walsh took the snap.

Calling the game and the pivotal play were Westwood One Radio's Tony Roberts and Tom Pagna. "How do you play this one, Coach?" Roberts quizzed Pagna. "Do you blitz or do you play it straight?"

"I think I have to play it man-to-man and get some pressure on him," Pagna answered. Roberts called the play, "(Dale) Dawkins wide to the right, Brown in the slot, Conley the wing-man on the right side. Three wide receivers right. They're going to go for two. Back to throw. Walsh looks…looks…looks…has the time…lobs the ball!" Walsh's pass soared. Miami's intended receiver, Leonard Conley, leapt into the air. And with a quick step in front of

Conley, Pat Terrell did the same. For a moment, football history seemed to be dangling in the balance—old vs. new, tradition vs. modern domination, heart vs. hype, "Catholics vs. Convicts."

"The pass is...batted down!" proclaimed Roberts, "It's batted down by Terrell!" With just the very tips of his fingers, Pat Terrell sent the ball harmlessly to the ground, securing the Irish victory and reaffirming Notre Dame's place in collegiate football history. "And the Irish—they win it this afternoon! They're out in front 31 to 30, as Jimmy Johnson went for two. Forty-five seconds left to go and Pat Terrell breaks up the two-point pitch that would have put Miami of Florida out in front!"

Cheers of triumph echoed again in Notre Dame Stadium like they hadn't in years. Notre Dame had avenged Miami's domination of the past and set the crown jewel in what would become a national championship season.

Ironically, Terrell and Conley knew each other well. Both hailed from the St. Petersburg, Florida, area, and had faced each other as rivals in high school. For that last play, instead of being in his running back position, Conley set up in the slot across from Irish defender Terrell. Terrell looked across the line of scrimmage right before the play and caught Conley's eye. "We just grinned," said Terrell, "and I had a feeling then that they might be looking to throw the ball his way."

When asked, "Where were you when Notre Dame beat Miami in 1988?" Irish fans young and old provide countless memories, yet the same feelings of elation and pride. As fans poured onto the field, Notre Dame players joined their fellow students and held their golden helmets high in salute and appreciation. Irish faithful across the nation knew once again what it felt like to be champions.

Even today, people will stop Terrell on the street to talk about his last-minute, game-saving leap. "There were fifty-nine thousand at that game that day," Terrell laughs, "and I think every single one of them over the last thirteen years has told me what they did or how they felt when I got that deflection. It gets kind of funny, but it still does mean a lot to me."

Appropriately, during the University's Century Celebration of Notre Dame Football in 1999, Pat Terrell's game-saving deflection was named the most memorable moment in Notre Dame football history.

For every fan watching that day, indeed it was.

Notre Dame faithful celebrate an emotional win against Miami on the field after the game.

The Eleventh National Championship

(left to right) Mike Heldt (55) and Tim Grunhard (75) celebrate a Rodney Culver score. ■ 1989 Fiesta Bowl program and ticket

As Notre Dame's top-ranked football team ran onto the field of Sun Devil Stadium on January 2, 1989, the Fighting Irish were looking to do more than write a fitting final chapter to a storybook season. The Fiesta Bowl, matching 11–0 Notre Dame against undefeated and third-ranked West Virginia, was to be the culmination of a voyage that had started when most of these Irish players were still in high school.

Though few realized it at the time, Notre Dame's march back to the top of the college football world began on November 30, 1985, in Miami's Orange Bowl. There, in Gerry Faust's final game as Notre Dame's head football coach, the University of Miami Hurricanes and head coach Jimmy Johnson humiliated the Irish 58 to 7. Amid the drubbing, former Notre Dame coach Ara Parseghian, providing expert analysis for the telecast of the game, predicted that the Irish would one day rise from the ashes of the debacle like the Phoenix of ancient mythology. Many viewers no doubt dismissed the claim as empty partisan bravado. After all, there wasn't much else Parseghian could say in surveying the shattered remnants of a program that he himself had rebuilt twenty-one years earlier.

It's not hard to imagine Parseghian had an inkling that Lou Holtz, named coach just three days earlier to clean up the wreckage, would be the right man for the enormous task ahead. Given Parseghian's great success at Notre Dame, he understood the spirit of Notre Dame better than most. Maybe Parseghian was even acquainted with the handful of young men who would lead Notre Dame's rebirth and fulfill his prophecy. Frank Stams was a sophomore, Andy Heck, Corny Southall, and Wes Pritchett were just freshmen on that November day against Miami in 1985. But three seasons later, they would be leaders on Notre Dame's remarkable 1988 team.

At the outset of the 1988 season, expectations were modest by Notre Dame standards. Holtz had wasted little time leading the Irish out of the wilderness during his first two seasons at Notre Dame. Holtz's first Irish team ended their season with a record of 5–6, and followed it up with a more promising 8–4 the next season. But as the 1988 season opened, he was faced with the prospect of replacing all five starters on the offensive line, plus Heisman Trophy winner Tim Brown. Prognosticators felt the Irish were still a year away from a legitimate shot at the national title and pegged the Irish deep in the second half of the preseason top-twenty polls.

(left to right) Coach Lou Holtz leads
his team in prayer before the game.
■ Holtz leads his team onto the field.

On the way to their date with West Virginia, the Irish had already extracted a measure of revenge from Miami, upsetting the top-ranked Hurricanes and snapping their sixteen-game winning streak. Notre Dame had exorcised another demon by emerging from the Los Angeles Coliseum, graveyard of so many Irish title dreams, with a 27 to 10 victory over second-ranked and previously unbeaten USC.

Given the depths to which the program had sunk earlier in the decade, the prospect of eleven victories in 1988 would have caused euphoria among the Irish faithful. But with each passing victory, the stakes kept getting higher. Now, under Tempe's overcast skies, a loss to West Virginia in this national championship matchup would undo all the accomplishments of an astounding season.

But unlike Parseghian, those forecasters overlooked the heart—and talent—of the Notre Dame players whose character was forged in the inferno of the Orange Bowl in November 1985. The 1988 Irish roster was also loaded with young talent—Tony Rice, Ricky Watters, Michael Stonebreaker, Todd Lyght, Patrick Terrell, Tony Brooks, Chris Zorich, Derek Brown, Raghib Ismail—and these players had neither the time nor the inclination to wait for another year.

But the Irish were ready for the spotlight. Not only was this Irish team light years away from the dispirited bunch that was steamrolled by Miami three years earlier, it hardly resembled the squad in the season opener, or even the heroic group that came within a two-point conversion of losing to Miami in October.

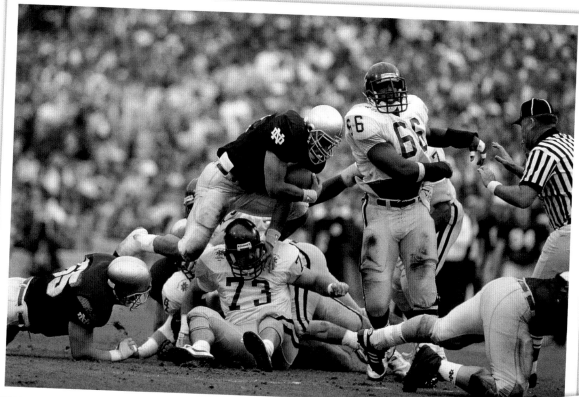

(left to right) A Notre Dame back dives over the Mountianeer defense. ■ Quarterback Tony Rice (9) evades tacklers.

A relentless defense set the tone early in the Fiesta Bowl, knocking Mountaineer quarterback Major Harris to the sideline with an injured shoulder on the third play of the game. Harris managed to return, but was limited to forty-two yards rushing and 166 yards passing. Then, Notre Dame quarterback Rice, who would end the day with 213 yards passing, hit tight end Derek Brown with a twenty-three–yard throw. "Down the middle…complete to the tight end, and it's Derek Brown all the way to the four-yard line!" shouted Dick Enberg, who along with Merlin Olsen, called the game on NBC Television.

"Derek Brown, 6' 7", 235, a brilliant first-year freshman…he is a star of the future!" proclaimed Enberg. Brown ran the ball to the four-yard line, and then running back Rodney Culver slammed it in for the score. "So, threatening to make it more than nine–nothing, they got a touchdown! Rodney Culver! Notre Dame scores again!" said Enberg. Following Reggie Ho's extra point kick, Notre Dame held a 16 to 0 lead early in the first half. Before the game was over, Rice would pass for two touchdowns and run for seventy-five yards, earning him offensive MVP honors. Harris joined

Miami's Steve Walsh and USC's Rodney Peete as highly-celebrated quarterbacks of undefeated teams victimized by Rice and the Irish defense.

The game's outcome was never in doubt as Notre Dame built a 23 to 3 second quarter lead. West Virginia's last gasp in the second half was snuffed out by Notre Dame's tenacious defense. Fittingly, two 1985 survivors played key roles. Following a touchdown to make the score 26 to 13 late in the third quarter, the Mountaineers intercepted Rice at the Notre Dame twenty-six. On first down, Flash Gordon dropped Harris for a two-yard loss. Cornerback

Stan Smagala broke up a Harris pass in the end zone on second down before Frank Stams and freshman linebacker Arnold Ale sacked Harris for a loss of twelve yards.

The Mountaineers, in field goal range when the drive started, had no choice but to punt the ball back to Notre Dame. The Irish promptly drove eighty yards. On third and goal, Enberg described Notre Dame's final blow. "Watters to the right…The fake…the throw…the touchdown! To Frank Jacobs," Enberg said with a slight tone of surprise, "who caught only one pass all year for Notre Dame. He's got one for a touchdown in the Fiesta Bowl!" Notre Dame led 34 to 13.

West Virginia added a consolation touchdown, but the Irish emerged triumphant, 34 to 21. Notre Dame had earned its eleventh national championship, and the first since the 1977 season.

Frank Stams, the only member of the 1988 team who was in the starting lineup in '85, personified the change in the luck of the Irish. As the starting fullback in '85 against Miami, Stams spent the game unsuccessfully attempting to eke out yardage against a smothering Miami defense. By '88, Stams was a first-team All-America defensive end, one of Holtz's several brilliant personnel shifts. Andy Heck was another beneficiary of Holtz's shrewd eye. After spending the 1987 season as Notre Dame's starting tight end, Heck moved to offensive tackle. His play was so dominating that he earned first-team All-America honors in his first year at tackle, going on to play for over a decade in the NFL.

(top to bottom) Lou Holtz directs the show from the sidelines. ■ Mountaineer quarterback Major Harris is tackled by a Notre Dame defender.

Mark Green lined up behind future Heisman Trophy winner Brown at flanker as a freshman in '85. He was Notre Dame's starting tailback for the next three years. Never, though, did Green get the chance to be the featured back among Holtz's deep and talented pool of running backs. Instead, he shared playing time, carries, and the spotlight with younger players.

"We had a ton of talent," remembers Green, who went on to play several years with the Chicago Bears. "It was a matter of putting yourself second. It was more important to me to help win a national championship with these guys at Notre Dame." That idea seemed preposterous during Green's first year at Notre Dame. Green and his classmates were the foundation for Holtz's brilliant rebuilding effort. Instead of being on the *Titanic*, they were on Apollo 11.

Highlighted by weekly victories over the No. 1, 2, 3, and 9 teams in the country, Notre Dame finished the 1988 season 12–0 and earned their record eleventh national championship. Fittingly, the Irish ultimately did make it to Phoenix, or at least nearby Tempe. And, true to Ara Parseghian's words, the Fighting Irish had risen from the ashes. "I started playing football when I was eight and played until I was thirty-one," Stams says. "That season was the most fun I ever had playing football."

The Rocket Takes Off

The veteran sportswriters who cover Notre Dame football are not easily impressed. Whether they hail from large media markets like New York or Chicago, or from just down the road in nearby Elkhart or Goshen, Indiana, they've seen it all. To them, there's always another supposed blue chipper in the pipeline, always another incomparable prospect, always another potential All-American heading into South Bend.

And so it was in 1988 when, as a true freshman, Raghib Ismail returned two kickoffs for touchdowns against lowly Rice University.

But it was a different story a year later on a dreary, rainy, Saturday afternoon in Ann Arbor, Michigan, on September 16, 1989. The game pitted defending champion and No. 1–ranked Notre Dame against coach Bo Schembechler's second-ranked Michigan Wolverines in a battle of traditional college football powerhouses.

There, the legend of the "The Rocket" was forged in the smithy of Michigan Stadium in front of 105,912 soggy, poncho-wearing fans, who had endured wind, rain, and cold while watching a true star shine. Now the writers strained for words to describe the electrifying nature of Ismail's performance, and in its next issue, *Sports Illustrated* would feature the "Rocket Man!" on its cover.

What did the 5-foot, 10-inch, 175-pound native of Wilkes-Barre, Pennsylvania, do to deserve such attention? Frankly, in the first half, nothing. The two heavyweight teams exchanged body blows on the rain-soaked artificial turf and went to the locker room at halftime with the Irish holding a precarious 7 to 6 lead.

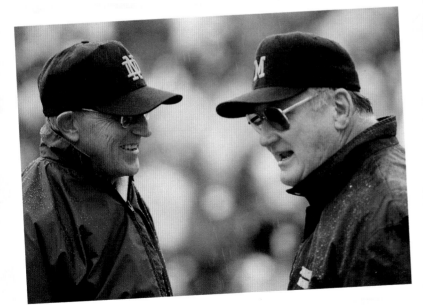

(left to right) Ismail eludes would-be Michigan tacklers on his way to the end zone. ■ Lou Holtz and Michigan coach Bo Schembechler ■ Game program and ticket from the September 16, 1989, game

As was his custom during his tenure at Notre Dame, coach Lou Holtz, upon winning the coin toss, elected to receive the second-half kickoff rather than the first. With the rain having stopped and the toothbrush turf drying out, it was time to see why Ismail had earned the nickname "Rocket" as an eighth grader.

The speedy Ismail had been a sprinter at E.L. Meyers High School in Wilkes-Barre and led his track team to two state titles, winning individual state titles in the 100-meters and the indoor 55-meters as a junior. In 1989, as a sprinter on Notre Dame's track team, Rocket captured the conference indoor title in the 55-meters and placed second in the men's 200-meter outdoor event.

Ismail took the kickoff at Notre Dame's eleven-yard line, started up the middle, and headed to the right. Calling the game on ABC-TV was veteran college football sportscaster Keith Jackson.

In his trademark staccato cadence, Jackson's excitement seemed to escalate with every yard of Rocket's amazing run, "Ismail up the middle. He…is…gone! Unless there's a flag behind him." Running upfield untouched, Ismail soared into the end zone a mere eleven seconds after he caught the ball. "No flags! Touchdown!" proclaimed Jackson, "They call him 'Rocket'…and you just saw why." In what seemed like an instant, Notre Dame took a 14 to 6 advantage. It was the first time since October 27, 1957—nearly thirty-two years—that anyone had returned a kickoff for a touchdown against Michigan.

"That guy is fast," Schembechler told the media following the game. "He may be the most dangerous football player in the country on the ground."

Schembechler evidently did not come to that realization until after he stunned Holtz, many in the crowd, and the press box by kicking to Ismail a second time following an Elvis Grbac–led Michigan touchdown drive that reduced the Irish lead to 17 to 12 with 12:58 to play.

"When Rocket went out to receive [the kickoff], I told him they would probably try to squib it and kick away from him," Holtz said. But Wolverines kicker Gulam Khan booted the ball high and deep, giving Ismail another opportunity. Holtz said he overheard one of his players who was standing behind him on the sidelines say, "Oh, here we go."

This time Rocket caught the ball at the Irish eight-yard line, headed upfield, and broke the opposite way. "It was a bigger hole this time and I saw a crease off to the left," Rocket recalled. At the twenty-five–yard line, Michigan's Brian Townsend hit him hard. "I felt somebody on my leg, but then I broke free." Again, ABC's Keith Jackson called it as Ismail charged for the end zone, "From the nine,

(opposite page, top to bottom) Ismail prepares to make a cut. ■ *The Rocket races downfield.*

Ismail outruns Michigan players in the rain.

Tony Rice attempted only two passes in the game, including a six-yard touchdown to Alonzo Johnson.

here he comes, Rocket! To the thirty! Here he goes! Good-bye!" This time, in what seemed like a heartbeat, twelve seconds elapsed from the moment Rocket caught the kickoff until he was in the end zone. Jackson shouted, "Touchdown Notre Dame!"

"Ninety-two yards! Eighty-nine yards! Give 'im the rest of the day off, Lou!" said Jackson in summing up Ismail's extraordinary pair of performances.

Following the conversion, the Irish were up 24 to 12. Grbac, also a sophomore, put up another touchdown for the Wolverines, making the final score 24 to 19,

but the Irish defense hung on. "We are supposed to find a crease," Ismail later told the no-longer-so-skeptical media. "Most of our kickoff returns we want to take it straight up where we catch the ball and form a wedge." Not that the wedge-makers would have to hold their blocks for very long.

"Our front line made the initial contact and created a decent-sized crease, and then the back wall in front of me surged through and picked up the guys who were left," Rocket recalled. "Rod Culver got the kicker and I had a clear route. It was nice." Just like that.

Holtz said he knew early on that Ismail was unlike any other player he had coached. "I said from the first day he walked out on our field in shorts he was special," Holtz said. "A lot of guys are trackmen who play football, but [he] is a football player who also runs track." Ismail made NCAA history by becoming the first player to return two kickoffs for touchdowns in two separate games, first against Rice and now against Michigan. Rocket rounded out his sophomore year by racking up an impressive average of 135.7 all-purpose yards per game, including 478 rushing yards on sixty-four carries, and 535 yards on twenty-seven receptions. He was named 1990 Orange Bowl MVP in a 21 to 6 victory over Colorado after rushing for 108 yards and scoring on a thirty-five–yard run. With five career kickoff returns for touchdowns, Rocket was just one short of setting an NCAA record. His career average of twenty-two yards per reception set a Notre Dame record.

(left to right) Ismail offers a quick prayer in the end zone. ■ *The Rocket takes off.*

Irish Win the "Cheerios Bowl"

Lou Holtz escaped the pressure of major college football on a calm December night in his adopted hometown of Orlando, Florida. The Notre Dame head coach left his team for the day to spend some time with his wife, Beth, and their children. He hoped to recharge his batteries for the upcoming Sugar Bowl contest against third-ranked Florida at the New Orleans Superdome in front a national television audience on ABC.

Holtz organized a family dinner at a favorite restaurant. There was little talk about Notre Dame's difficult final three games of the regular season—two demoralizing losses and a flawed victory over Hawaii. The Irish had allowed a staggering 112 points in the three games. Notre Dame plummeted from No. 5 in the national rankings to No. 18.

Holtz was upbeat and optimistic, and he told his family that he felt his team was poised to beat the highly ranked Gators, despite being a virtually unprecedented eighteen-point underdog. "We couldn't be better prepared," he said.

Then, as legend has it, the waiter appeared at the table. "Aren't you Lou Holtz, the Notre Dame coach?" he asked.

Holtz replied that he was.

"Let me ask you a question. What's the difference between Notre Dame and Cheerios?"

The only thing sharper than Holtz' winning percentage at South Bend was his wit, so he knew where the waiter was going. But he played along. "I don't know," he said.

"Cheerios *belong* in a bowl."

In early November, Notre Dame was ranked No. 5 with a gaudy 8–1 record. But then the Irish blew a twenty-four-point lead in a home loss to Tennessee, lost by three touchdowns at Penn State, and barely escaped Hawaii with a 48 to 42 victory. Nonetheless, they were extended a Sugar Bowl bid. What's more, there was internal strife within the program. It was rumored widely in the media (and, more dangerously, in the privacy of the Notre Dame football locker room) that Holtz had tired of Notre Dame and that Stanford coach and NFL coaching legend Bill Walsh was poised to step in.

(left to right) Sugar Bowl MVP Jerome Bettis lifted the Irish to victory rushing for 150 yards. ■ Bettis rushes for one of his three fourth-quarter touchdowns. ■ Game program and ticket from the 1992 Sugar Bowl

(left to right) Tailback Rodney Culver breaks through the line for his first touchdown. ■ Bettis celebrates his first TD in the fourth quarter ■ Bettis and quarterback Rick Mirer (3) celebrate Bettis' third touchdown.

"I'm not going to bust my ass out there," one player was reported to have said amidst all the turmoil. "I'm going to wait until Bill Walsh comes in."

But the Cheerios comment had a galvanizing effect on the Irish. "We have nothing to lose," Holtz told his team. "No one believes you should be here, no one wants you to be here. But we can win."

Holtz knew that trickery and masterful motivation would need to be involved.

First, he ordered new uniforms—white jerseys with green numbers with matching green socks. "I just felt it was a special occasion with the adversity we went through at the end of the year," Holtz said. "It seemed like the Lady on the Dome would forgive us for wearing green."

Next, Holtz took over the defense from embattled defensive coordinator Gary Darnell. He told the media that the Irish would pressure Florida quarterback Shane Matthews with a variety of blitzes. The reality was just the opposite. Holtz inserted a "junk defense" for the pass-happy Gators that sometimes had nine Irish defenders in pass coverage.

Finally, Holtz unleashed "The Bus." In a performance that served as an effective preview to an outstanding NFL career, Notre Dame fullback Jerome Bettis rushed for 150 yards.

With under five minutes left in the game and Notre Dame trailing 22 to 17, Jerome Bettis suddenly broke open the game, and became a Notre Dame legend in the process. At first and goal, quarterback Rick Mirer fired a three-yard pass to Bettis, who marched in for a touchdown. "First and goal…and Bettis scores the touchdown!" proclaimed Al Michaels, who led the team coverage for ABC along with Frank Gifford and Dan Dierdorf.

The two-point conversion put the Irish ahead 25 to 22, and about a minute later Bettis broke loose

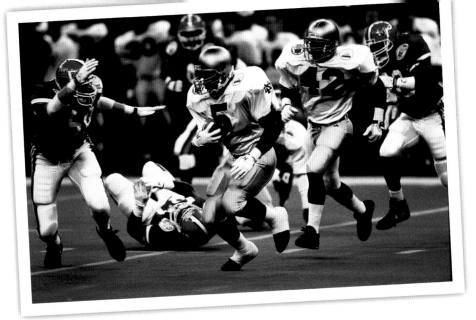

again. Averting Florida's nine-man front line, Bettis barreled forty-nine yards to the end zone. Again, Michaels called it, "Here goes Bettis!…All the way for a touchdown, Notre Dame!" Notre Dame now led 32 to 22.

With 2:28 to play, Florida rallied with a touchdown, but missed the two-point conversion opportunity. Regaining possession with the score now at 32 to 28, Irish fullback Ryan Mihalko blew a hole in the Gator defense allowing Bettis to plow through and sprint thirty-nine yards for his third and final touchdown in less than three minutes. "They give it to Bettis!… He picks up the first down again…and… a…touchdown!" shouted Michaels. "Un–be–liev–able!" added Dierdorf. Notre Dame had stunned Florida with a 39 to 28 victory.

"My man, Jerome Bettis," Holtz cooed later. "That is an outstanding football player."

Rick Mirer, who would be the No. 2 pick in the NFL draft in April 1993, completed fourteen of nineteen passes for 154 yards in Holtz's balanced, controlled offense. Bettis simply dominated, and finished with a flourish. The harried Matthews—college football's most prolific quarterback that season—had thirty incomplete passes and nightmares of green shamrocks.

"It was insane," said linebacker Justin Goheen. "Florida was able to march on us for a while, but every time they got within the twenty, they couldn't complete the damn pass because there were so many people from Notre Dame in coverage. Holtz stepped in and did some amazing coaching."

"We didn't just fool Florida," said defensive stalwart Pete Bercich. "We fooled the media. We manipulated them the whole month before the game."

The postgame talk was not only about breakfast Cheerios, but also about how Holtz had Florida head coach Steve Spurrier for lunch. "He outfoxed him," said Goheen. No longer was Holtz a candidate for burnout. He and the program were re-energized.

"I didn't realize how important this victory was," Holtz said the next day, "just as we enter recruiting and the winter program."

Holtz knew where to give the ultimate credit for the victory.

"When they blew the game's final whistle," Holtz said, "the first person I thought of was that waiter. I had the most satisfying image of him sitting at home, crying in his Cheerios."

Notre Dame went 21–1–1 in its next twenty-three games over two seasons and was ranked in the top five for fourteen weeks. It was the last great run of the Holtz era and, for that matter, Notre Dame football in the twentieth century.

(top to bottom) Culver turns upfield. ■ The elated Irish carry Holtz off the field.

The Snow Bowl:
Penn State vs. Notre Dame

On any other November day, it would have been regarded simply as a minor snow flurry, an insignificant precipitation unworthy of an after-thought by the residents of a north central Indiana town well versed in the unrelenting wrath of the "lake effect" snow.

But this was not just any other November day. It was one of those magical Notre Dame football Saturdays in South Bend. And this was not just any other opponent. It was Penn State and its living legend of a coach, Joe Paterno, against the Fighting Irish and one of Paterno's great coaching rivals, Lou Holtz.

This was also not just any other game between these two preeminent college football programs. It was the final meeting in a seventeen-game series that pitted this small, private, Catholic, liberal arts institution in the Midwest against a sprawling, state-sponsored, land grant university in the East. Different as they were, both schools shared a passion for college foot-ball and a commitment to playing the game at the highest level with players who were expected to excel both in the class-room and on the field.

Giving it even more significance, the contest also was the final home game for NFL-bound Irish, including quarterback Rick Mirer, fullback Jerome Bettis, tailback Reggie Brooks, defensive lineman Jim Flanigan, line-backer Demetrius DuBose, punter/place-kicker Craig Hentrich, offensive lineman Aaron Taylor, tight end Irv Smith, and defen-sive back Jeff Burris. For them, this was their last chance to play the game they loved in the place they loved.

And so the flurries could not be dismissed. In the context of all the finality and football significance that accompanied this game, the swirling snow flakes assumed an almost sacramental aura, drifting down on "The House That Rockne Built" and bless-ing the sell-out crowd and its gridiron heroes with nature's frozen holy water.

Picturesque as the gently falling snow looked to the national TV audience watching on NBC, it created abominable field conditions typical of past games between the Irish and the Nittany Lions. The cleat-clinging mud, the cold-hardened and slippery

(left to right) Quarterback Rick Mirer barks out the signals. ■ Coaching legends Holtz and Paterno chat before the game. ■ November 14, 1992, game program and ticket

(clockwise from bottom left) Notre Dame fans take shelter from the storm. ■ Snow swirls down on the final home game of 1992 at Notre Dame Stadium. ■ Stadium crews work valiantly to keep the field clear.

pigskin, and the swirling stadium winds all conspired with the teams' respective tough defenses to make the game a field goal contest well into the second half.

The game was tied at nine midway into the fourth quarter, but Penn State took a 16 to 9 lead after recovering an Irish fumble and converting for a touchdown. Now, with just 4:19 to play and history looking on with an arched eyebrow, the Irish took over on their own thirty-six–yard line needing seven points to tie and eight to win.

Aaron Taylor recalls, "It was do or die. The seniors' last home game. Rick Mirer at the helm. Guys like Reggie Brooks, Jerome Bettis, and the other linemen. Everybody knowing we could do it."

As the senior quarterback led his team onto the field for what turned out to be the defining moment of his Notre Dame career, Mirer stopped cocaptain DuBose on his way to the sideline and told him, "We're going to do this."

On the first play of the drive, Mirer's pass was deflected and nearly intercepted. It was anything but an auspicious start. But things turned around quickly. Mirer marched the Irish downfield, completing a twenty-one–yard pass to Jerome Bettis to Penn State's forty-two, then scrambling for fifteen yards on second and sixteen. A seventeen-yard pass and a seven-yard scramble brought the Irish to the Penn State eight. On first-and-goal, Mirer handed off to Brooks, who was taken down, at the four-yard line. On second-and-goal, Mirer gained a yard. On third down, he threw to a sliding Brooks. The pass was incomplete and the clock stopped.

Now, with twenty-five seconds remaining, it was fourth-and-goal from the three-yard line, and two storybook plays were about to unfold that would make it a game for the ages.

Tony Roberts and Tom Pagna called the game on Westwood One Radio. Roberts summed up the critical situation for the Irish, "You want to talk about

(top to bottom) A thundering collision at the top of the pile ■ The Notre Dame defense suffocates the Penn State ground game.

crunch time?…The moment of truth?…Here it is!" Notre Dame launched a play normally reserved for two-point conversion attempts, and Roberts described the setup on the field, "Dawson wide to the left. Griggs in the slot. Irv Smith, the tight end, right. Flanked to the right is Reggie Brooks. One running back—Jerome Bettis."

Mirer took the snap, drifted back to pass, and looked to his primary receiver, Smith, who was covered by Nittany Lions defenders. "Go!" Mirer yelled, signaling Bettis, who had stayed in the back-field to block, to loop underneath the Penn State pass coverage and head straight for the end zone. A Penn State linebacker went left, Bettis went right, and Mirer delivered the ball. "Touchdown, Notre Dame! Jerome Bettis and a touchdown!" proclaimed Roberts. The stadium erupted. "He is mobbed in the end zone!" The Irish now trailed the Lions by only one, 16 to 15.

(left to right) Bobby Taylor and Jeff
Burris try to block Penn State's kick.
■ Jerome Bettis (6) follows his blocks.

Earlier in the season, Holtz came under sharp criticism for settling for a 17 to 17 tie with Michigan. This time, there was no doubt. The Irish were going for two points and the victory.

In the huddle, Mirer vowed to his teammates, "I'm not going down with the ball in my hands." Again, announcer Tony Roberts described the formation, "Three wideouts left. One out to the right…" Mirer was alone in the backfield with receivers to either side. He took the snap. "Back to throw Mirer…" He looked left, scanned to the right, nothing. Scanned further right, nothing. "Looks…looks…looks…." Mirer began to sense Penn State defenders surging toward him. "Rolls to the right. Pump fakes…"

Mirer escaped a would-be tackler and spotted Brooks in the back of the end zone. "Throws the ball!…It is caught!…Reggie Brooks! Reggie Brooks got it for a two pointer! And Notre Dame is out in front 17–16 with twenty seconds left!" Roberts shouted.

"I kind of drifted across and when I saw Rick scrambling, I just took off," Brooks said. "The play wasn't really designed for me to go way across, but when the quarterback scrambles, you have to work to get open."

Mirer's pass barely cleared the outstretched arms of Penn State rusher Rick McKenzie, but it found its

(clockwise from top left) Bettis is wrestled to the ground by the Penn State defense. ■ Tailback Reggie Brooks runs alone in the flat. ■ Holtz looks on through the snow.

way into the arms of the 5-foot, 8-inch Brooks, who stretched out in the end zone. After a miraculous catch, he fell to the ground just inside the sideline, giving Notre Dame its final 17 to 16 margin. It was only the second reception of the year for tailback Brooks, who was Mirer's fourth option on the play.

"Reggie sometimes does not catch the ball on weekdays, but he makes it count on Saturdays," Mirer said. "I wouldn't have thrown it if I didn't think he had a chance to catch it."

Without hesitation, Mirer recently recalled the excitement of that career-defining comeback against Penn State, "I've never had a better feeling in football than when Reggie Brooks caught that pass."

Wooden Bats Away Charlie Ward and No. 1 Seminoles

Disc 2 • Track 15
November 13, 1993

At the time, it might have been the most surprising invitation any member of the college football media had ever received.

It happened two days before the second-ranked Fighting Irish were to host No. 1 Florida State at storied Notre Dame Stadium in a contest with such an over-the-top level of pregame hype that it gave new resonance to the phrase "Game of the Century." Both perennial powers had 9–0 records and sixteen-game winning streaks.

Notre Dame coach Lou Holtz was known neither for ostentatious demonstrations of overconfidence nor for any abiding affection for the press. In the days preceding this monumental game, one would have expected the man who annually professed fear of facing the U.S. Naval Academy—which hadn't beaten Notre Dame since the '60s—to be fretting about the vaunted Seminoles and their roster of future NFL draft choices. Holtz had one national title on his résumé, his old rival Florida State head coach Bobby Bowden didn't, yet Holtz saw Bowden as the media darling.

Nonetheless, just forty-eight hours before one of the biggest games of his life, Holtz invited a group of the overflow national sports media that had converged on South Bend to his house for a catered rib dinner.

And the only thing more remarkable than the invitation itself was Holtz's demeanor at the soirée. "He was remarkably calm, remarkably hospitable," said Joe Tybor, Irish beat reporter for the *Chicago Tribune*. "I had covered the team for four years and this was the first time he had ever invited the media to his home. He had a smile and a confidence that I had never seen before."

"Everybody was saying, 'What's with Lou, what's gotten into Lou?'" Tybor recalls. "And every reporter

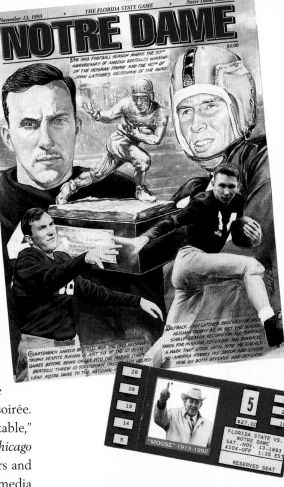

(left to right) Wooden (22) leaps into the air to knock down Ward's pass.
■ Lou Holtz leads the pregame charge.
■ November 13, 1993, game program and ticket

Wooden Bats Away Charlie Ward and No. 1 Seminoles ▼ ND 131

(clockwise from bottom left) Florida State's Warrick Dunn (28) runs deep in Notre Dame territory. ■ Florida State's Kez McCorvey (88) hauls in a Charlie Ward pass in front of Notre Dame's Bryant Young (97). ■ Adrian Jarrell (10) runs with blockers in front of him.

walked away from his house that night saying, 'Lou knows something.'"

The battle began with psychological warfare. Florida State players toured Notre Dame Stadium wearing green baseball caps with a gold interlocking FSU on the front and shamrocks on the side. They mocked the Notre Dame mystique and claimed never to have heard of anyone named "Rock Knut-nee." They indicated they knew nothing, and cared less, about Notre Dame's football tradition.

But in playing host to the sports media just before what many viewed as college football's de facto national championship game, Holtz won the battle of one-upsmanship. And his team was a six and one-half point underdog.

As it turned out, Holtz did know something. "He really felt that they were small," said Kevin McDougal, who started—and starred—at quarterback all season. "They were really fast, but he thought we just had to pound them and then come back and throw."

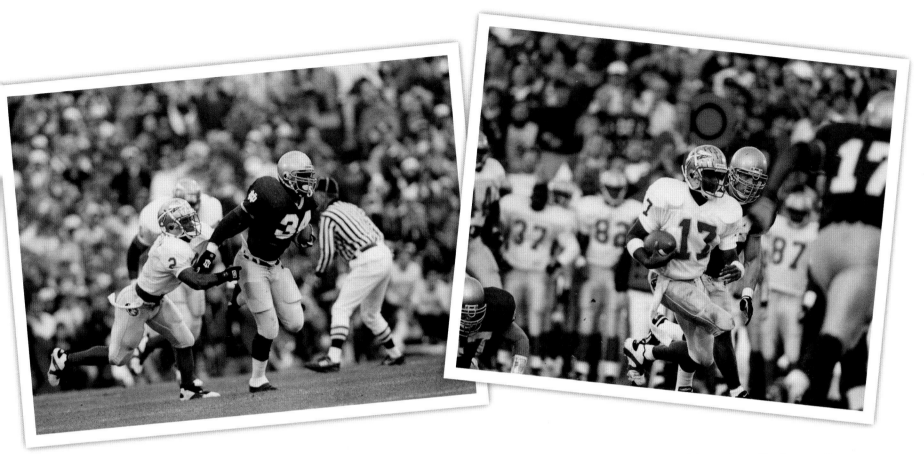

In front of a capacity crowd at Notre Dame Stadium, and a national television audience watching on NBC, Notre Dame pounded away on Florida State. After the Seminoles' Heisman Trophy candidate Charlie Ward engineered a touchdown drive on the game's opening possession to give FSU a 7 to 0 lead, the Irish running game took over. Center Tim Ruddy, tackles Aaron Taylor and Todd Norman, and guards Mark Zataveski and Ryan Leahy (grandson of legendary Irish coach Frank Leahy), simply bulldozed the speedy but lighter Seminoles.

"There were massive holes there for me," said Notre Dame tailback Lee Becton, who rushed for 122 yards and one touchdown. "The offensive line was moving people back five yards." Previous Florida State opponents had managed an average of only ninety-seven rushing yards per game against the Seminoles. The Irish ran for 238 yards. "We did kinda overpower them," said Becton, who ran for a twenty-six–yard touchdown early in the second quarter.

While the teams clashed on the field, the fans were doing their best to overpower each other in a battle of the chants. Every time the Florida State fans would break into their war chant, Irish fans, who stood in nervous excitement for nearly the entire game, drowned them out with their chant of "Louuuuu!"

Notre Dame abused Bowden's boys relentlessly in the first half and went to the locker room with a 21 to 7 lead. Ironically, Bowden later confessed to giving a Rockne-esque halftime locker room speech, reminding them "they had been behind by that much with a quarter to go before, and won," and that if Notre Dame scored twenty-one points in a half, they could too.

"Coach Holtz felt that beating teams bad would come back to haunt you someday," McDougal said. "He would run the clock out instead of have us keep doing what we were doing. Michigan and Florida State almost came back and beat us."

(left to right) Fullback Ray Zellars breaks away from a Florida State defender during the first quarter. ▪ Quarterback Charlie Ward took matters into his own hands, driving the ball to the four-yard line with less than three minutes left on the clock.

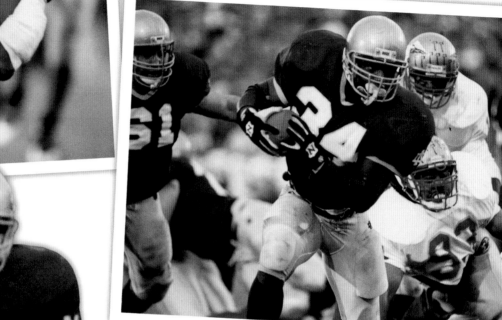

(clockwise from bottom) Lee Becton rushed for 122 yards and a touchdown. ■ Becton is pursued by two Florida State defenders. ■ Notre Dame's Ray Zellars drives through a hole for big yardage.

A forty-seven–yard field goal by Kevin Pendergast, the longest of his college career, and an eighty-seven–yard touchdown drive put the Irish up 31 to 17 with just over three minutes left in the game.

But Holtz's second half conservative offensive plan nearly backfired as the brilliant Ward led the Seminoles back. On first and goal with 3:04 left on the clock, Ward, unable to find a clear receiver, ran the ball himself to the four-yard line. But a dead ball foul was called against Jesus Hernandez, costing the already time-challenged Seminoles fifteen yards.

"The perfect season for the Seminoles, coming down to this play," said NBC's Charlie Jones as he summed up the critical moment. "It is fourth down and goal to go, twenty-yard line, 2:31 left." In determined fashion, Ward dropped back and fired into the end zone. The ball was nearly intercepted by Notre Dame's Brian Magee before it landed into the grateful hands of Seminole Kez McCorvey. "And the drama continues!" Jones said in amazement. The twenty-yard touchdown pass capped a forty-five–yard drive and hope sprung once again from the Seminoles sideline as the Irish lead was cut to seven.

The Notre Dame offense quickly went three and out, and a shanked punt gave the Seminoles the ball back near midfield with a scant fifty-one seconds left in the contest.

Three complete passes by Ward, first to star running back Warrick Dunn, then the next two to McCorvey, put FSU on the Irish fourteen with three seconds to play. Notre Dame took a timeout.

"This is a moment that memories are made of," said Charlie Jones. "National title on the line for Florida State, it's also there for Notre Dame, it's within the grasp of either ball club." The timeout ended and both teams took the field. Ward dropped back to throw his fiftieth pass of the day. Shawn Wooden was among six Notre Dame defensive backs covering the end zone. "My job was to read Charlie," said Wooden.

Ward rolled left, looked to Warrick Dunn in the end zone, and fired. Before the ball was within three yards of Dunn, Wooden stepped in front of him and broke up the pass. "Knocked down by Wooden! Notre Dame wins, 31–24!" shouted Jones. "The

ghost of Knute Rockne is living and he is smiling!" And the celebration began.

After the game, Holtz complemented the indomitable spirit of both teams, "This I think was just a great football game…it's one game that lived up to all the hype." Holtz went on to say that the Seminoles team was the best Notre Dame had beaten since he became coach. "They didn't respect the lady on the dome at all," said Irish defensive tackle Bryant Young. "There's a special spirit here that does exist. I know that now after what happened today."

Notre Dame swapped positions with Florida State, becoming No. 1 in the AP ranking. Holtz's pregame hospitality scheme didn't set any new social trends, but he certainly demonstrated his winning flare for wooing pundits while pulling off one the biggest upsets of the year.

(left to right) Notre Dame players and fans unite to celebrate the victory.
■ *Jubilant Irish fans cover the field in the wake of Notre Dame's defeat of No. 1–ranked Florida State.*

The Notre Dame Spirit

...:03, :02, :01.

Time has expired, and the game is now another chapter in the epic story of Notre Dame football. Maybe you were fortunate enough to have seen a ball batted away in the last minute of the game to secure an Irish victory, or a catch in the end zone by an unlikely target. Maybe your cheer added to the roar that gave the kicker that last bit of energy to barely clear the crossbar for a last-second, game-winning field goal. However it may have happened today, the Fighting Irish, in their own spirited way, were victorious. And you shared in it.

Before leaving the field, the players assemble to salute their classmates in the north end zone, holding their battered, golden helmets high above their heads in celebration and appreciation. The students and fans answer with a roar of song and cheer. They part by joining together and singing "Notre Dame, Our Mother," as the band plays for the last time of the day.

Game programs are left curled in the seats, the covers slightly dampened by the constant twisting of hands, or they are carefully tucked into pockets and bags like treasured heirlooms, proof of attendance at another of Notre Dame's great games.

Now, students parade en masse back to campus to continue their celebration. The players take a few moments in the locker room and reflect on what they shared on the football field. You join with the other fans pouring out of the stadium and maneuver your way through the remnants of the weekend's tailgate celebrations. You see a father walking from the stadium hand-in-hand with his son. What a day it was. And as you glance back, the sun is setting beyond the Dome, reflecting a red-orange glow across the inspired yet serene campus.

But something lingers. You can't put your finger on it, but you feel it in your heart. Call it Notre Dame "spirit."

What is the spirit of Notre Dame football, the spirit that is so often credited with the collective joy of those who embrace it? If you ask Notre Dame's alumni or subway alumni, its students or parents, its fans or faculty, its players, coaches, or even visiting teams, they all inevitably come to the same conclusion. That it's difficult to put in words exactly what that "spirit" is.

It's spirit that binds tradition with tomorrow, unites alumni and students with distant fans, many of whom will never have the chance to travel to South Bend and sit inside the "The House That Rockne Built" to

(clockwise from left) The Fighting Irish prepare for battle. ■ A Notre Dame greeting card produced in 1939 ■ Notre Dame students and fans turned out in droves to welcome their national champion Irish home in 1949.

(top to bottom) Bagpipers perform
on campus to stir up Irish pride.
■ The Irish Guard leads
the band through campus.

see a game. Spirit is what makes today's simple, joyous game part of tomorrow's treasured memories.

Certainly, all the legend and lore of one of the most celebrated collegiate sports teams of the twentieth century adds to the Notre Dame experience. But the Notre Dame spirit permeates well beyond its fabled stadium. In fact, the stadium is only one of many spirit-filled places on a campus where prayers are uttered and answered, and where miracles seem routine.

Notre Dame has an extremely unique spiritual atmosphere for a modern, national university. Fittingly, most visible on the Notre Dame campus are a statute of the Virgin Mary atop a brilliant golden dome, a huge library mural of Jesus surrounded by followers, the magnificent Sacred Heart Church, and the candlelit stone Grotto, a replica of the grotto at Lourdes, France, where Mary is said to have appeared to a young French peasant girl in 1858.

Surely, most great universities boast picturesque landscapes, athletic traditions, extravagant tailgating celebrations, and beloved fight songs. But the common bond for fans of most football teams often begins as mere geography. You don't root for Notre Dame because it's close or because it bears the name of the state in which you live. Followers are linked by spirituality and a history that's woven into each of its nooks and crannies, into every class and every class reunion, into its songs and its memories.

Like its small acreage tucked away on the quiet lakes of St. Joseph and St. Mary's, Notre Dame's heritage was born humbly enough from visions of a French priest landing in the Indiana prairie. Its founder, Father Edward Sorin, could hardly have predicted the unparalleled national devotion and international sphere of influence his dream, his tribute to "Our Lady," would bring.

Perhaps those around him in Notre Dame's most tragic hour witnessed the birth of the school's legacy for overcoming odds great and small. In 1879, thirty-seven years after its founding, much of the campus, including the Main Building, burned to the ground. Standing amidst his life's work reduced to ashes, Fr. Sorin addressed a tightly knit community inside the Sacred Heart Church.

"There was absolute faith, confidence, resolution in his very look and pose," said Professor Timothy Howard of the scene. "'If it were all gone, I should not give up,' were Sorin's words in closing. The effect was electric. It was the crowning moment of his life. A sad company had gone into the church that day. They were all simple Christian heroes when they came out. There was never more a shadow of a doubt as to the future of Notre Dame."

And so, a culture of dedication and resolve brought acclaim to nearly every facet of Notre Dame's people and programs. Its coaches are revered as national celebrities, and its fight song is known throughout the world. Its athletes have been favorites and underdogs, giants and giant-killers, legends and unsung heroes inspiring literature and movies. Its presidents counseled United States presidents, and one of Sorin's successors, Father

Theodore Hesburgh, was instrumental in the drafting of the country's Civil Rights legislation. One of the most evident results of Sorin's legendary determination, Notre Dame's football program has achieved prominence like no other—leading all colleges in numbers of Heisman Trophy winners, national championships, and graduation rates of its players.

"I never cease to be amazed at the constant devotion and unfailing spirit that ND inspires in its followers," heralded former Irish quarterback Joe Montana once observed.

It would be difficult to match the unique and rich history of Notre Dame football and the collective experience of her coaches, players, students, and fans. Perhaps in time, in terms of wins, numbers of great players, great coaches, or championships, her achievements will be surpassed. Admittedly, these

Irish fans show their enthusiasm by holding signs (top) or, in some cases, surfing the crowd (right).

are just football games in which young men take part.

But somehow, because of the miraculous results of many of these gridiron classics, whether you saw them from the stands or in your living room, they meant something more. You remember exactly who you were with and exactly how you felt. You remember how, with the other kids in the neighborhood, you ran that winning play over and over in your front yard. Or how you hugged and kissed your sweetheart after that winning touchdown. Or high-fived your best buddy proclaiming, "Can you believe this!?" Just when it didn't seem possible, the Irish made one last play for victory.

And again you are convinced that something else, be it luck, confidence, history, or something greater…something else was there, inspiring the Irish.

(top to bottom) The Fighting Irish cheerleaders fire up the crowd. ■ Notre Dame players pay homage to the fans at every home game by raising their helmets to the stands.

Over the past century, Notre Dame football has created a solid foundation for another hundred years of great moments, and then some. More important, however, are the memories of family and friends, of loyalty and faith, of commitment to team and to personal, individual excellence that both Notre Dame, the place, and Notre Dame, the team, provides.

And although it's exciting to awaken the echoes and relive the thrilling moments of the past, the spirit of Notre Dame is both responsible for, and reveals itself through, the entire, rich, and consistently successful history of her football program. In that way, football at Notre Dame is more than a game. And at no time is the Notre Dame spirit more evident than on gameday.

(clockwise from top right) Members of the Irish Guard raise the flag before the game. ■ The Irish Guard performs at Notre Dame stadium. ■ The Irish Guard stands at attention.

(top to bottom) The Irish celebrate a
hard-fought victory. ■ Notre Dame
students congratulate their team
after the game.

Afterword
by Joe Theismann

Coming out of high school in South River, New Jersey, I knew where I was going to college—North Carolina State. I was fortunate enough to have had my choice of nearly one hundred colleges. But I had finally called a halt to my whirlwind recruiting season.

Or had I?

Notre Dame, knowing my decision, nevertheless asked me to please make one more trip to South Bend.

Now, I wasn't Catholic. I didn't have any family members telling me, "You must go to Notre Dame." It was just another school, no big deal.

But I went for that second visit. When I returned, my dad, meeting me at the airport, asked, "Well, what do you think?" I told him, "I'm going to Notre Dame." He asked, "Why?" And I told him, "I can't give you a specific reason."

It wasn't solely because of my visits there, or because of the legend and mystique of Notre Dame.

Rather than me choosing the university, it was almost like the university chose me. It seemed like there was another element in the universe saying, "This is the place for you." It was like I was predestined to go to Notre Dame.

At first, it certainly didn't appear that I could fulfill my quarterback dream at Notre Dame. I was coming to a team led by

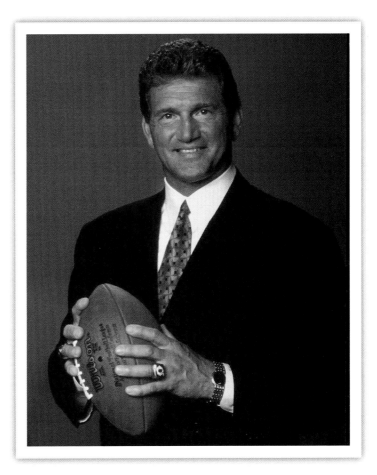

Terry Hanratty, a returning quarterback good enough to be a Heisman Trophy candidate. Add to that the fact that I was only 5 feet, 10 inches, and 152 pounds, and was one of thirteen freshmen quarterbacks heading into camp. It might have seemed I had made the wrong choice after all.

But I wasn't discouraged. I came in one week ahead of the other twelve quarterbacks and got a jump start on learning the offense. By working hard and studying, I wound up being the starting quarterback at Notre Dame by the end of my sophomore season. To me, that still sounds unbelievable.

My third game as the starter came against the University of Southern California at the Coliseum in Los Angeles. On our first pass play from scrimmage, I threw a pass that was intercepted and run back for a touchdown. When I came to the sidelines, I told our coach, Ara Parseghian, "Don't worry, I'll get it back." He later said he knew at that moment he had made the right decision in selecting me.

While Coach Parseghian gave me a chance to make a name for myself, it was the school's sports information director, Roger Valdiserri,

who determined what that name would be. Mr. Valdiserri summoned me to his office before the start of my senior season and asked me a very odd question. "How do you pronounce your last name?"

"It's Thees-mann," I said. He answered, "No it's not. It's Thighs-mann." "It's Thees-mann," I insisted. Mr. Valdiserri began to explain that he felt that I had a real chance to win the Heisman Trophy. By changing the pronunciation of my last name to rhyme with Heisman, he thought I would increase my chances of winning.

I felt better about it after talking to my grandmother, Eva, who informed me that the correct pronunciation of our family name, which is German, was closer to "Thighs-mann" than "Thees-mann." So I went along with Mr. Valdiserri's idea, and even though I lost the Heisman Trophy to Jim Plunkett that season, I still remained Joe "Thighs-mann."

The most memorable game I played for Notre Dame came in my senior season, again versus Southern Cal at the Coliseum in Los Angeles. I passed for a school record 526 yards in a driving rainstorm. But my most memorable moment at Notre Dame didn't even come on the football field. Instead, it came in a building we called "the Cow Palace," the building our basketball team played their games in on campus.

The occasion was the pep rally that was held prior to our leaving for the Southern Cal game my senior year. The school wasn't yet coed in those days, so you had seven thousand crazed drunks, mostly guys screaming and hanging from the rafters.

Out walks Pat O'Brien, the actor who played Knute Rockne in the movie, Knute Rockne, All-American. And he starts reciting Rockne's famous pep talk. Those seven thousand Notre Dame fans were suddenly stone silent. You could have heard a pin drop. Once he finished, not only was the team ready to run through a wall, but everyone in the building would have followed.

Right then and there, I understood the magnitude of the tradition and the history of the University of Notre Dame. I understood the mystique.

With every passing season in the thirty years since I played for Notre Dame, I have grown more and more appreciative of the quality it has over every other university. For players and fans, there's nothing quite like the great legacy that is Notre Dame football. And I truly hope the experience of reading this book, and listening to the sounds of the games on these CDs, passes on the powerful feelings of that great legacy.

I've been in a Super Bowl and I've played in front of a hundred thousand fans, but nothing in my twelve-year NFL career ever compared to running out on the field at Notre Dame Stadium. It felt like my feet never touched the ground. To this day, I still get goosebumps just talking about it.

#7

Acknowledgments

There are so many people to whom I owe special thanks for their unique and invaluable contributions to this book.

My deepest gratitude to my publisher, Dominique Raccah, for her vigilant determination in making the vision a reality.

A special thank you to Todd Stocke, editorial director at Sourcebooks, for his enthusiasm, dedication, creativity, and editing talents. Once again, he's proven to be the best. Thank you to the talented staff at Sourcebooks for their boundless creativity that has resulted in this wonderful book. Special thanks to editor Alex Lubertozzi for his tremendous efforts and to the entire editorial team, especially Jennifer Fusco, Peter Lynch, Amy Baxter, Kelley Thornton, and Andy Logemann.

The production and design staff went above and beyond. Thanks to Norma Underwood, Maricel Quianzon, Micah Taupule, Taylor Poole, Megan Dempster, Tressa Minervini, Molly Benefield, and Dawn Weinfurtner.

I am extremely grateful to Regis Philbin for lending the perfect voice to this book, a voice that resonates with genuine passion and love for the university and awakens the echoes of the true spirit of Notre Dame.

My sincerest gratitude to Martin Sheen for breathing life into the written words of Grantland Rice, allowing the Four Horsemen to ride once more.

A special thank you to Ara Parseghian and Joe Theismann for their unique perspectives as a coach and 9-a player at the University of Notre Dame. This book is richer for their insights, and I am honored by their contributions.

I am profoundly grateful to the University of Notre Dame, specifically the generous and enthusiastic cooperation of John Heisler, director of Sports Information, and his staff, including Lisa Nelson and Carol Copley, who always seemed more than happy to answer our myriad questions; to Charles Lamb, Marlene Wasikowski, George Rugg, and the rest of the staff of the University of Notre Dame archive for their gracious hospitality during my visit, and their tireless efforts and thoroughness with all of the follow-up work; to Dick Conklin, Chuck Lennon, Dennis Moore, and Larry Williams for their enthusiasm and guidance throughout the project.

I am extremely grateful to Maura Kelley. Her invaluable qualities of conscientiousness, insightfulness, resourcefulness, and wonderful positive outlook have made my job infinitely easier, and going to work a joy.

My heartfelt thanks to Debbie Dolins, publicist to Regis Philbin. The recording of Regis's narration was made even more enjoyable by her skillful diplomacy and conscientious coordination. And thank you to Jim Griffin at the William Morris Agency for his guidance during the project.

A special thank you to Tony Zirille (class of 1989), Ed Sullivan, III (ND law school class of 1993), and his sister, Kelly Sullivan (class of 1983). Their genuine love of Notre Dame and passion for its football history fueled my inspiration to do this book.

I am grateful to Taylor Richards, Sean Stires, and Casey Daniels of WNDV-FM for their encouragement and support from the very beginning.

My sincerest gratitude to Larry Michael of Westwood One Inc., Louise Argianas of ABC Sports, Deanna O'Toole of CBS Sports, and Chris Ottati of NBC Sports for their invaluable cooperation that permitted me to include the broadcasts of these thrilling and memorable Notre Dame moments.

Thank you to Tony Roberts and Al Wester for their enthusiastic support of this book, and for giving voice to many of Notre Dame's most thrilling moments that will echo forever in the hearts and imaginations of Notre Dame fans everywhere.

My gratitude to Dick Lynch, class of 1958 and Notre Dame star running back, for sharing his insights and the excitement of the unforgettable 1957 Notre Dame victory over Oklahoma.

Thank you to John Miley for contributing portions of his Notre Dame football broadcast collection, and for his unequaled passion to preserve sports broadcast history.

A special thank you to Adria DeBaca of the Pasadena Tournament of Roses, Rick Baker of the Southwestern Bell Cotton Bowl Classic, Courtney Morrison-Archer of the Orange Bowl Committee, Jeff Hundley and Gregory Blackwell of the Nokia Sugar Bowl, and Lisa Arias of the Fiesta Bowl for their assistance in providing many wonderful photographs.

My sincerest gratitude to Ed Sullivan (class of 1957 and a cocaptain for the Fighting Irish) and his family for including me in what was my first, and hopefully not last, Notre Dame tailgate party, an experience made especially memorable by their warm hospitality, delicious homemade mostaccioli, and wonderful stories of past Notre Dame glories.

I am extremely grateful to Joe Doyle, former sports editor for the South Bend Tribune, and Jeff Jeffers, sports anchor for WNDU-TV, South Bend, Indiana, for generously sharing their vast and expert knowledge of Notre Dame football history.

Thank you to Bill Farmer and Larry Roberts for contribut-ing their rare Notre Dame memorabilia that helped make this book complete.

Thank you to Karen Carpenter at Sports Illustrated, Mike Bennett at Lighthouse Imaging, Heather Marsh-Rumion at Corbis Images, Carolyn McMahon at AP/Wide World Photos, Jim Lee at Allsport Photography, Rosa Di Salvo at Archive Photo, Joe Raymond, and Don Stacy for their diligence and dedication in providing us with the very best photographs.

Thank you to John R. Lovett from the Western History Collection of the University of Oklahoma, Mary O'Brien and Edward Galvin from the Syracuse University Archive, Jana Drvota from the Ohio State University Photo Archive, Paulette Martis from the Sports Information Department of Michigan State University, and Taylor Watson from the Paul W. Bryant Museum of the University of Alabama, for providing photographs from their collections.

As always, thank you to Marc Firestone for his counsel, encouragement, and friendship, and to Bill Kurtis for lending his voice to the first of my multimedia books, and for his continued gracious support.

Thanks to Jack Kelly, the "hound of heaven" and a true son of Notre Dame, who inspires me through his zest for life, his kindness, and his strong commitment to his faith.

The most special thank you goes to my wife, Colleen, my son, J.B. (James), and daughter, Jillian, for their love, support, and understanding; to my parents, Jim and Betty Garner, for their love and encouragement; and to the rest of my family and friends for their love and support throughout.

Finally, a special thank you to Janel Syverud for her diligence in keeping my business organized; Dan Kavanaugh, Cynthia Helmer, Meloney Hudson, Bradley Warden, Corrie Gorson, Stuart Richardson, Justin Hixon, and everyone at Mirage Productions for their support, friendship, and encouragement.

Credits

Text and research editorial team:

Tony Zirille, Editorial Consultant (class of '89). "Thank you to those with whom I've shared these great moments. My grandpa Mike, a stadium usher for forty-six years, and my grandma Josephine, who's a testament to what the faith and spirit of Our Lady really means. My wife Joy, and my little boys, with whom I look forward to sharing many years of ND football games together. And to my dad, Frank ('64), who taught me how to love Notre Dame."

Kelly Sullivan

Craig Chval

Barry Cronin

Tim Bourret

Alan Teuli

Paul Feinberg

David Haugh

Bill Moor

Nick Grimmer

Audio editorial team:

Narration written by Mark Rowland, writer/producer of television documentaries.

Archival audio and audio research provided by John Miley, The Miley Collection, Evansville, Indiana, the finest sports broadcast archive in the world.

Additional audio research services provided by Steve Cohen, Jeff Jeffers, and Bill Pikus.

Audio credits:

Regis Philbin was recorded at National Video Center, New York, NY.

Martin Sheen was recorded at The Audio Department, New York, NY.

Audio production engineering by Mike Forslund. Engineering production assistant Nancy Forslund.

Some audio segments have been edited for time and content.

Archival audio provided by and copyright of:

ABC Sports Inc.

CBS Sports Inc.

NBC Sports Inc.

Westwood One Radio Networks Inc.

Ronald W. Reagan Presidential Library

University of Notre Dame Archives

WNDU-TV, Notre Dame, Indiana

WSBT-TV, South Bend, Indiana

The music score used in "Notre Dame Spirit" is titled "Call to Glory," by Hughes Hall and Jeff Lamont. Published by Xtend Music (ASCAP).

Announcers

Special thanks also to the broadcasters who brought excitement to these moments. They are:

Bill Stern	Al Wester
Joe Boland	Van Patrick
Curt Gowdy	Don Criqui
Jim Gibbons	Lindsay Nelson
Tony Roberts	Paul Hornung
Tom Pagna	Paul Alexander
Chris Shenkel	Tom Hedrick
Keith Jackson	Al Michaels
Dick Enberg	Frank Gifford
Merlin Olson	Dan Dierdorf
Jay Randolph	Frank Glieber
Paul McGuire	Connie Alexander

Photo Credits

All credits listed by page number, in the order indicated on pages.

Every effort has been made to correctly attribute all the materials reproduced in this book. If any errors have been made, we will be happy to correct them in future editions.

Page i University of Notre Dame Sports Information Department **Page ii–iii** Lighthouse Imaging **Page iv–v** Mackson/Sports Illustrated **Page vi–vii** Don Stacy **Page xii** McDonough/Sports Illustrated **Page xviii** AP/Wide World Photos **Gameday** 2 University of Notre Dame Sports Information Department; 3 University of Notre Dame Archive; 4 University of Notre Dame Archive; 5 University of Notre Dame Archive; 6 University of Notre Dame Archive; 7 University of Notre Dame Archive, University of Notre Dame Archive; 8 University of Notre Dame Archive, University of Notre Dame Archive, University of Notre Dame Archive; 9 University of Notre Dame Archive, University of Notre Dame Archive; 10 University of Notre Dame Archive, University of Notre Dame Archive, University of Notre Dame Archive, University of Notre Dame Archive; 11 Lighthouse Imaging, Lighthouse Imaging, Lighthouse Imaging **Knute Rockne, All American** 12 University of Notre Dame Archive; 13 Corbis/Bettmann; 14 University of Notre Dame Archive, Corbis/Bettmann; 15 Corbis/Bettmann, Corbis/Bettmann; 16 Corbis/Bettmann; 17 University of Notre Dame Archive, University of Notre Dame Archive, University of Notre Dame Archive; 18 University of Notre Dame Archive, University of Notre Dame Archive; 19 Archive Photos, Archive Photos **The Four Horsemen** 20 Archive Photos; 21 University of Notre Dame Archive; 22 University of Notre Dame Archive, Pasadena Tournament of Roses, University of Notre Dame Archive; 23 University of Notre Dame Archive, University of Notre Dame Archive **The Original "Game of the Century"** 24 University of Notre Dame Archive; 25 University of Notre Dame Archive, Larry Roberts; 26 Ohio State University Photo Archive, Ohio State University Photo Archive; 27 Ohio State University Photo Archive, Ohio State University Photo Archive **A**

Heisman History 28 Downtown Athletic Club of New York City, Inc.; 29 Downtown Athletic Club of New York City, Inc., Downtown Athletic Club of New York City, Inc.; 30 University of Notre Dame Archive, Downtown Athletic Club of New York City, Inc.; 31 Downtown Athletic Club of New York City, Inc., University of Notre Dame Archive; 32 Downtown Athletic Club of New York City, Inc., Downtown Athletic Club of New York City, Inc., University of Notre Dame Archive; 33 Downtown Athletic Club of New York City, Inc., Downtown Athletic Club of New York City, Inc., Corbis/Bettmann; 34 Downtown Athletic Club of New York City, Inc., Corbis/Bettmann, Downtown Athletic Club of New York City, Inc.; 35 Downtown Athletic Club of New York City, Inc., Corbis/Bettmann; 36 Corbis/Bettmann, Downtown Athletic Club of New York City, Inc.; 37 Downtown Athletic Club of New York City, Inc., Don Stacy; 38 All Sport, Downtown Athletic Club of New York City, Inc. **Notre Dame Ends Oklahoma Winning Streak** 40 University of Notre Dame Archive; 41 Western History Collections/University of Oklahoma Libraries, Bill Farmer, Larry Roberts; 42 Western History Collections/University of Oklahoma Libraries, Corbis/Bettmann; 43 University of Notre Dame Archive, Western History Collections/University of Oklahoma Libraries **The Great Irish Coaches** 44 University of Notre Dame Sports Information Department, University of Notre Dame Sports Information Department, Joe Raymond, Jonathan Daniel/Allsport; 46 AP/Wide World Photos, AP/Wide World Photos; 47 AP/Wide World Photos, AP/Wide World Photos; 48 Archive Photos, Joe Raymond; 49 University of Notre Dame Archive; 50 AP/Wide World Photos, Lighthouse Imaging; 51 AP/Wide World Photos, AP/Wide World Photos **Perkowski Kicks Twice** 52 Syracuse University Archive; 53 University of Notre Dame Archive, University of Notre Dame Archive **10-10 Tie for the National Championship** 54 Michigan State University; 55 Michigan State University, University of Notre Dame Archive, Larry Roberts; 56 Chicago Sun-Times, Chicago Sun-Times, Chicago Sun-Times; 57 Drake/Sports Illustrated, Michigan State University, Corbis/Bettmann, Sports

Illustrated **Theismann Runs Over No. 1 Texas** 58 AP/Wide World Photos; 59 University of Notre Dame Archive, University of Notre Dame Archive, University of Notre Dame Archive; 60 Southwestern Bell Cotton Bowl Classic, AP/Wide World Photos; 61 Southwestern Bell Cotton Bowl Classic, Sports Illustrated, University of Notre Dame Archive **The Trojan War** 62 Don Stacy; 63 Corbis/Bettmann; 64 Corbis/Bettmann, Corbis/Bettmann; 65 Corbis/Bettmann, Corbis/Bettmann; 66 University of Notre Dame Archive, University of Notre Dame Archive, Kluetmeier/Sports Illustrated; 67 Kluetmeier/Sports Illustrated, Kluetmeier/Sports Illustrated; 68 University of Notre Dame Archive, University of Notre Dame Archive, Joe Raymond; 69 Joe Raymond, University of Notre Dame Sports Information Department; 70 Joe Raymond; 71 Lighthouse Imaging, Lighthouse Imaging; 72 Lighthouse Imaging, Lighthouse Imaging; 73 Joe Raymond **Clements and the Irish Beat 'Bama** 74 Clarkson/Sports Illustrated, University of Notre Dame Archive, University of Notre Dame Archive; 75 Joe Raymond, University of Notre Dame Archive, University of Notre Dame Archive; 76 Nokia Sugar Bowl, Nokia Sugar Bowl; 77 Nokia Sugar Bowl, Nokia Sugar Bowl, Nokia Sugar Bowl **End of an "Ara"** 78 AP/Wide World Photos; 79 Orange Bowl Committee, Larry Roberts, Larry Roberts; 80 Orange Bowl Committee; Paul W. Bryant Museum/University of Alabama, Orange Bowl Committee, Orange Bowl Committee **Rudy** 82 Rudy Ruettiger; 83 University of Notre Dame Archive, University of Notre Dame Archive; 84 University of Notre Dame Archive, Archive Photos, Archive Photos; 85 University of Notre Dame Archive, Rudy Ruettiger **1978 Cotton Bowl** 86 Sports Illustrated; 87 Southwestern Bell Cotton Bowl Classic, University of Notre Dame Archive, Larry Roberts; 88 Iooss/Sports Illustrated, Sports Illustrated; 89 Southwestern Bell Cotton Bowl Classic, Corbis/Bettmann, Cooke/Sports Illustrated **Montana's Chicken Soup Heroics** 90 Corbis/Bettmann; 91 University of Notre Dame Archive, University of Notre Dame Archive; 92 Southwestern Bell Cotton Bowl Classic, Southwestern Bell Cotton Bowl Classic, Southwestern Bell Cotton Bowl Classic; 93 University of Notre Dame Archive, Southwestern Bell Cotton Bowl Classic **Harry O' Gets the Call** 94 University of Notre Dame Archive; 95 Joe Raymond, University of Notre Dame Archive, University of Notre Dame Archive; 96 Joe Raymond, Joe Raymond, Joe Raymond; 97 Joe Raymond, Joe Raymond, Joe Raymond **Irish Upset No. 1 Pitt** 98 Lighthouse Imaging; 99 Donald J. Stetzer/Pittsburgh Post-Gazette, University of Notre Dame Archive, Bill Farmer, Bill Farmer; 100 Albert M. Hermann/Pittsburgh Post-Gazette, Albert M. Hermann Jr./Pittsburgh Post-Gazette; 101 Marlene Karas/Pittsburgh Post-Gazette, Marlene Karas/Pittsburgh Post-Gazette **Miami 1988** 102 Lighthouse Imaging; 103 Don Stacy, University of Notre Dame Archive, University of Notre Dame Archive; 104 Lighthouse Imaging, Lighthouse Imaging, Lighthouse Imaging; 105 Lighthouse Imaging, Lighthouse Imaging; 106 Lighthouse Imaging, Don Stacy; 107 Lighthouse Imaging **Eleventh National Championship** 108 Lighthouse Imaging; 109 University of Notre Dame Archive, University of Notre Dame Archive; 110 Lighthouse Imaging, Akers/Fiesta Bowl; 111 Jeff Kida/Fiesta Bowl, Lighthouse Imaging; 112 Lighthouse Imaging, Lighthouse Imaging; 113 Akers/Fiesta Bowl, Clarkson/Sports Illustrated, Biever/Sports Illustrated **The Rocket** 114 Biever/Sports Illustrated; 115 Don Stacy, University of Notre Dame Archive, University of Notre Dame Archive; 116 Lighthouse Imaging, Lighthouse Imaging; 117 Sports Illustrated; 118 Biever/Sports Illustrated; 119 Lighthouse Imaging, Lighthouse Imaging **The Cheerios Bowl** 120 AP/Wide World Photos; 121 AP/Wide World Photos, University of Notre Dame Archive, University of Notre Dame Archive; 122 Strohmeyer/Sports Illustrated, Strohmeyer/Sports Illustrated, Tielemans/Sports Illustrated; 123 University of Notre Dame Sports Information Department, University of Notre Dame Sports Information Department **The Snow Bowl** 124 Lighthouse Imaging; 125 Lighthouse Imaging, University of Notre Dame Archive, University of Notre Dame Archive; 126 University of Notre Dame Archive, University of Notre Dame Archive, University of Notre Dame Archive; 127 Lighthouse Imaging, Lighthouse Imaging; 128 Lighthouse Imaging, Lighthouse Imaging; 129 Lighthouse Imaging, Lighthouse Imaging, Lighthouse Imaging **Wooden Bats Away Ward** 130 Clarkson/Sports Illustrated; 131 Clarkson/Sports Illustrated, University of Notre Dame Archive, University of Notre Dame Archive; 132 Joe Raymond, Lighthouse Imaging, Joe Raymond; 133 Joe Raymond, Joe Raymond 134 Joe Raymond, Joe Raymond, Joe Raymond; 135 Clarkson/Sports Illustrated, Lighthouse Imaging **Notre Dame Spirit** 136 Lighthouse Imaging; 137 Corbis/Bettmann, University of Notre Dame Archive; 138 Marlene Wasikowski, Marlene Wasikowski; 139 Iacono/Sports Illustrated, University of Notre Dame Sports Information Department; 140 Lighthouse Imaging, Lighthouse Imaging; 141 Lighthouse Imaging, Lighthouse Imaging; 142 Lighthouse Imaging, Lighthouse Imaging, Lighthouse Imaging; 143 Lighthouse Imaging, Lighthouse Imaging; 144 Lighthouse Imaging **Afterword** 146 University of Notre Dame Archive

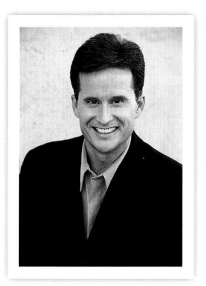

JOE GARNER is the *New York Times* bestselling author of *And The Crowd Goes Wild*, *And The Fans Roared*, and *We Interrupt This Broadcast*. A twenty-year veteran of the radio business, his expertise on the media's coverage of major sporting and news events has been featured on *Larry King Live*, *Weekend Today*, CNN, and NPR's *Morning Edition*. Garner's books were also bestsellers in the *Wall Street Journal*, *Publishers Weekly*, and *USA Today*.

REGIS PHILBIN is the Emmy Award–winning host of the hit television shows *Who Wants to Be a Millionaire* and *Live with Regis and Kelly*. He is a Notre Dame alumnus and received an honorary doctor of laws degree for his contributions to Notre Dame and South Bend.

Also by Joe Garner

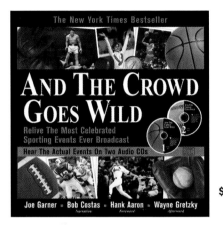

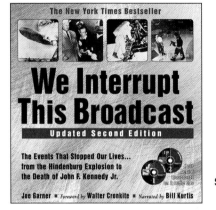

**$49.95 hardcover with
2 audio CDs**

AND THE CROWD GOES WILD

In words and images—and on two audio CDs narrated by Bob Costas—the acclaimed bestseller *And The Crowd Goes Wild* brings to life 47 spine-tingling moments that brought us to our feet. Two CDs contain two hours of audio, including the actual calls.

**$49.95 hardcover with
2 audio CDs**

WE INTERRUPT THIS BROADCAST

Updated to include the shocking and terrifying events of the past two years, *We Interrupt This Broadcast* brings to life the famous and infamous moments of the twentieth century with memorable audio, vivid photographs, and compelling text.

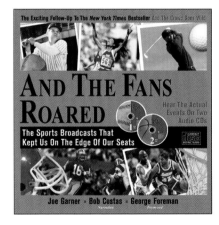

**$49.95 hardcover with
2 audio CDs**

AND THE FANS ROARED

Featuring the riveting stories that bring you back to the moment, acclaimed sports photographs, and two audio CDs narrated by award-winning sports journalist Bob Costas, *And The Fans Roared* delivers more than 40 of the most electrifying sports moments ever broadcast.

**$94.99
4 audio CDs**

BOXED SET

Own both *And The Fans Roared* and *And The Crowd Goes Wild* in a beautiful leather case. A perfect gift for the ultimate sports fan.